OLYMPIC OVAL
ANNEAU OLYMPIQUE

The Fastest Ice in the World™, Celebrating our 25-year legacy
Published to mark the celebration of the Olympic Oval's 25th anniversary season
Copyright © September 2013, The Olympic Oval, University of Calgary
ISBN 978-0-88953-369-1

Care has been taken to verify information and trace ownership of copyright material
contained in this book. The publisher will gladly receive any information that will enable
them to rectify any reference or credit line in subsequent editions.

Cataloguing data available from Library and Archives Canada

The Olympic Oval
University of Calgary
2500 University Drive NW
Calgary, Alberta, Canada T2N 1N4

oval.ucalgary.ca

Printed in Canada

The Fastest Ice in the World™

Celebrating our 25-year legacy

Leah Lacroix • Gillian Richmond • Tracy Stewart

Welcome

The Olympic Oval is a place where dreams come true. I have been a part of this "home" since 1988.

I remember when the idea of an indoor Oval was being talked about, and I didn't know if this could really ever happen! Skate in a covered oval? Wow! Coming from cold Saskatoon, I thought that would be a novelty!

I came to Calgary and skated in the building every few weekends leading up to the 1988 Olympic Games. I then came to watch the Games. The next September is when I qualified for the national team, and I spent the next sixteen years training at the Oval. Throughout the years, I came to realize that not only did the Oval have the best ice in the world, but had the best programs and the best people! I liked the people so much, I married one of them! My husband, Bart, was an ice-maker at the facility for 17 years.

The Olympic Oval isn't just about helping athletes reach the podium and realizing their dreams. It is also about the public – it is about introducing them to sport, to skating and to getting active. The Oval is about action – there are always things going on – whether it is the Dinos hockey team practicing, public skating on the oval, learn to skate on the rink, or Varsity athletics on the track, the Oval is always buzzing.

The Oval has had a unique energy since day one, and continues to have an energy that inspires. The stories from the last 25 years are sure to make you smile, cry, and want to put on your skates and skate fast!

Catorina Le May Doan
Associate Director, Olympic Oval

This 25th anniversary book is a legacy that will present a glimpse of the many successes and accomplishments at the Olympic Oval.

Thank you to all the staff for the countless hours involved in compiling information to produce this "Best Ever" coffee table book chronicling the history of this great facility. This book represents everyone who has been a part of the Oval Family over the years and everyone who has embraced our spirit of excellence. I hope you take time to reflect on the passionate milestones portrayed here, and the memorable moments that we were not able to include in the book, but live within us forever.

To all who will share these stories with your family and friends, it is because of you that the flame of the 1988 Olympics and the Olympic Oval will continue to burn bright as we move on to celebrate the next 25 years.

To the University of Calgary, Winsport (CODA) and the Government of Canada, thank you for the foresight in setting up the legacy funding that allows the Oval to operate and maintain its world class reputation.

The Oval is a building of concrete, metal and piping, but it is the collective heartbeat of the dedicated athletes, staff, volunteers and supporters who make it so much more, and make us the envy of every other Olympic legacy facility in the world.

Finally, my deepest gratitude to the directors, staff, volunteers and athletes who came before me and set our pathway to success, and to future athletes, volunteers and staff who will be the next leaders and champions of this great place. Your vision, dedication and inspiration is the foundation on which our legacy is built.

Kameron Kiland
Director, Olympic Oval

Intro

"Speed skating was an outdoor sport and now is an indoor sport...The Olympic Oval... completely transformed speed skating."

– Roger Jackson

They want a *what!?*

The idea to build a covered oval emerged out of Calgary's bid for the Winter Olympics and the vision for an expanded Faculty of Physical Education at the University of Calgary.

78 Shortly after Roger Jackson was recruited as Dean for the Faculty of Kinesiology (formerly the Faculty of Physical Education) at the University of Calgary (U of C) in 1978, he received a visit from Frank King (Calgary Olympic Development Association chairman). King wanted Jackson to help put together Calgary's third bid to host the Olympic Winter Games. Being the previous director of Sport Canada, Jackson was the logical choice to partner with King to spearhead this monumental task.

Dr. Roger Jackson, OC

In the beginning, Roger said no, as he had his hands full with his new role as Dean, but King persisted and eventually the two came together to bring the Games to Calgary. Bob Niven (Olympiques Calgary Olympics '88 vice-chairman) initiated this bid with King and Bill Warren (Canadian Olympic Association member and vice president of Bobsleigh Canada) joined them.

Roger Jackson saw the bid as an opportunity to expand the Faculty of Kinesiology and a chance to build a covered speed skating oval. After the experience with the artificial-ice outdoor oval, built for the 1975 Canada Games in Lethbridge, it was apparent this type of facility was a necessity. The speed skating events in Lethbridge were plagued with wind, dirt and dust blowing on the ice. Shadows on the ice surface, varying temperatures and snowfall were a challenge for facility and competition organizers, competitors, coaches and spectators. The funding to add a roof to the speed skating track in Lethbridge could not be secured and the bid for the 1988 Winter Olympics was an opportunity to rectify this situation...although not without its challenges.

Resistance to building a covered oval came on a few fronts. There was concern from the international skating community who were hesitant to move an outdoor sport indoors. There was also concern that this would set an expensive precedent and that the bulk of major events would be awarded to North America instead of Europe. In Canada, there was debate about the expense. An outdoor oval would cost $5-million and a covered oval would come in at an estimated $40-million. There was the issue of who would pay for ongoing operating costs, particularly for year-round use. And finally, there were differing opinions about where the facility should be built. Several locations were considered, including North Glenmore Park, Canada Olympic Park and the U of C.

In the end, Roger's idea for the Oval, the Faculty of Kinesiology and the U of C was realized. The idea was accepted by all parties, including the University, for an integrated facility that could take advantage of academic research and sport medicine. Being connected to light rail transit was also an important consideration. The use of the facility was for three specific communities: 1/3 high performance sport, 1/3 university and 1/3 public. This three-pronged model remains to this day.

Finally, with the agreement for the 1988 Winter Olympics complete, the bid committee ensured there would be ongoing operating and capital replacement funding for the Oval by establishing an Olympic endowment fund. This money was set aside to benefit three key Calgary Winter Olympic sites – the Olympic Oval, the Canmore Nordic Centre and Canada Olympic Park. By the end of the 1988 Games this fund totalled close to $90-million. In the 25 years since, this fund has grown substantially and until recently, was sufficient to ensure operations at all sites.

The construction site of the Oval was nicknamed "Jackson's Hole", in honour of the visionary behind the project. Once the construction was complete, the name evolved to "The Raj Mahal".

Calgary Wins the Bid

On September 30, 1981, Calgary won the bid to host the 1988 Winter Olympics.

The vote was conducted by the International Olympic Committee (IOC) in Baden-Baden, West Germany at the 84th IOC Session and 11th Olympic Congress. Calgary beat out the Italian resort city (and host of the 1956 Winter Olympics) Cortina d'Ampezzo in the first round and Falun, Sweden in the second round. The final IOC vote was 48-31 for Calgary. Calgary first tried to win a bid for the Winter Olympics in 1964, and again in 1968, but was defeated by Innsbruck, Austria and Grenoble, France respectively.

Calgary spent $2.5-million over three years preparing the bid. It was reported that Calgary put on one of the slickest, most complete demonstrations the IOC had ever seen. In addition to three years of intensive lobbying to secure the bid, the day prior members of the Calgary Olympic Development Association (CODA) held a free pancake breakfast for about 1,000 people at a national flower show in Baden-Baden. CODA president Bob Niven said, "They know we are from the West and they want us to put our cowboy hats on." CODA officials used the breakfast as an opportunity to showcase Calgary's culture and western hospitality.

Ready ... Funding in Place

The architectural model for the covered speed skating oval was unveiled on October 9, 1984 at the official signing of the funding agreement between the University of Calgary (U of C) and the Government of Canada for the 1988 Olympic Winter Games.

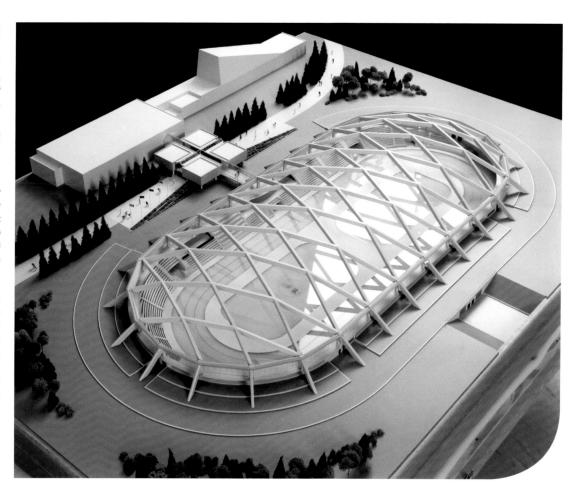

 U of C president Norm Wagner and Otto Jelenik, Minister of State for Fitness and Amateur Sport, were brought together for the ceremony where the $35-million contribution was announced. The agreement was that the federal government would finance 100% of the costs to build the Olympic Oval and the provincial government would fund 100% of the costs to build the adjoining kinesiology complex, the new athlete dormitories on campus, and renovate McMahon Stadium – all owned by the university.

Plans for the Olympic Oval changed considerably from when the initial Calgary bid was presented to the IOC in September of 1981. At first, the facility was planned as a traditional outdoor oval, but with the willingness to cover it, should the International Skating Union (ISU) approve such a plan. These discussions on design were encouraged by Jean Heckley, an ISU Board member who was also an architect in Paris. Because of the decision to build the Oval on the University of Calgary campus, and Roger Jackson's persistent vision for a covered facility, the design changed.

The university wanted a venue that met the aesthetic qualities of the rest of the campus. The architectural challenge posed to Calgary architects was to create a wide enough roof span to cover the ice surface and leave a wide border for portable spectator seating. The idea for this huge facility was that it would be more than just a single-purpose skating oval. Instead it would serve as a multi-purpose venue for the community to enjoy year-round.

Under Construction

The Olympic Oval was the first 400-metre covered speed skating oval in North America and the process of getting it built on a tight budget was a challenging task for the architects and engineers.

 84 The Oval was proposed as a multi-purpose venue with skating in the winter months and a field house (including artificial turf for football, soccer, lacrosse, and field hockey) in the summer. After one season with artificial turf installed it was apparent the logistics of installing the grass were prohibitive and the plan was quickly scrapped.

The roof of the building was (and still is) the focal point of the structure. Its design was both functional and architectural. The conceptual design needed to work within the parameters of a very tight budget and the structural design needed to provide maximum height over the playing surface while meeting safety code. It was decided that a design with a large number of small repetitive elements (using locally available materials) was the optimal solution. Arches are one of the oldest architectural forms and intersecting arches – like those on the Oval's roof – ensure long-term structural stability in any climate.

Mar. 11, 1985
- Construction begins. Over 300 concrete piles installed. Piles were 1.2 metres in diameter and extended 8 metres below grade. Size of piles was determined on-site through lateral load testing.

Aug. 1985
- First buttresses erected. Each buttress can carry thrust of 2-million pounds.

Sept. 1985
- Canadian men's national speed skating team visits the construction site for the first time.

Dec. 17, 1985
- First of perimeter roof beams installed.

Jan. 20, 1986
- Final perimeter roof beams installed. All beams installed in one month.

Feb. 1986
- First roof arch segment installed with scaffolding. Scaffolding supported the total weight of the roof arch segments – 8.5-million pounds.

Mar. 27, 1986
- Final intersecting roof arch segment installed. High strength, semi-lightweight concrete.

Apr. 1986
- Post-tensioning of arches. A total of 55 kilometres of cable used. Arches pre-compressed by stretching post-tension cable.

THIBAULT ILLUSTRATORS

Jun. 17, 1986
- Removal of temporary roof scaffolding starts. Towers lowered one at a time, 31 in total, each supporting 300,000 pounds. The first arch only dropped 4.3 centimetres.

Jul. 7, 1986
- Final scaffold support removed.

Aug. 1, 1986
- Steel roof decking installation begins.

Dec. 4, 1986
- Oval surface final concrete pour. The final pour of the concrete was continuous and lasted 20 hours. Another 30 hours of finishing time was required for the concrete as well as 28 days of wet-curing.

Mar. 1987
- Roof exterior complete. 12,000 porcelain panels were installed.

Jun. 1987
- Landscaping.

Sunday, Sept. 27, 1987
- Opening Day!

Construction Facts

- 400-metre oval ice surface, 13 metres wide and approximately 1/4 of a mile in circumference
- Covers 26,000 square metres, measures 200 × 90 metres, and is made of 21,000 cubic metres of concrete
- Two international sized ice surfaces (30m × 60m)
- 2,500 permanent spectator seats
- 4,000 temporary spectator seats
- 450-metre, two-lane running track
- 110-metre, eight-lane sprint track
- Long jump pit
- Pole vault box
- High performance weight room
- 60 square metres of stretching mats
- Air duct system to control airflow and building temperatures
- Boardroom and lounge for staff meetings, press conferences and athlete study area
- Three ice resurfacing machines
- Boom lift to access the light and air fixtures
- One forklift for moving equipment

The Roof
- 25.91 metres high, 12,000 roof panels. 160,000 rivets pulled out and replaced with screws and washers after 1988. Each screw head was painted by hand.

Seating
- Olympic Games – 2,200 permanent spectator seats, 4,300 removable seats, for a total of 6,500 seats for speed skating fans.

- 2013 – 2,000 permanent seats and 900 removable bleacher seats, plus additional removable seating can be installed when required.

Total Project Cost
- $39.9-million

Fun Fact
Why do speed skaters go faster at higher altitudes? Higher altitudes have less air density – about a 3% reduction for every 1,000 feet. This can result in faster speeds due to less aerodynamic drag.

A Grand Opening

National and international visitors, athletes, coaches, staff, faculty, families and the U of C community gathered to celebrate the occasion. Being the first covered speed skating oval in North America, the Oval was set to offer public skating, public running, hockey, speed skating competitions, special events and year-round training for speed skaters and high performance athletes. Juan Antonio Samaranch, the president of the International Olympic Committee officially opened the building, commenting that the facility was one of the "best" he had ever seen.

The Olympic Oval was part of an expanded physical education facility and included several structures: a seven-lane 110-metre running track; a high performance weight-lifting centre; a recreational fitness centre; 17 squash and racquetball courts; an outdoor centre and climbing wall; and a world-class gym with seating for 4,500 for volleyball and basketball. The very significant addition of the sport medicine centre was also part of this expansion.

Cathy Priestner Allinger was named the first general manager and the Oval opening team was put in place. As the general manager, Cathy Priestner Allinger set the foundation and framework for the Oval as a year-round training centre for high per-formance athletes and established a culture that quelled the fears of the Oval becoming obsolete.

The grand opening was the beginning for a facility that became a home for many. A place that would see world records smashed and one that would witness many local, national and international successes and personal triumphs. A place that would soon cement its reputation for having The Fastest Ice in the World™. One highlight of the opening ceremonies was a tribute to the provinces, signalling what the Oval would ultimately become – a home to speed skaters from across the country and eventually a home to high performance athletes from across the globe.

Dignitaries present at the opening ceremonies:

- **The Honourable Otto Jelenik**, Minister of State for Fitness and Sport

- **Dr. Norman Wagner**, President, The University of Calgary
- **Dr. Roger Jackson**, Dean of The University of Calgary Faculty of Kinesiology (formerly the Faculty of Physical Education) and President of the Canadian Olympic Association

- **Frank King**, Chairman, Olympic Organizing Committee
- **Bill Warren**, Chairman, Calgary Olympic Development Association
- **Honourable David Russell**, Deputy Premier, Government of Alberta

- **Ralph Klein**, Mayor, City of Calgary
- **His Excellency, J.A. Samaranch**, President, International Olympic Committee
- **Cathy Priestner Allinger**, General Manager, Olympic Oval

- **The Right Honourable Joe Clark**, Minister of External Affairs, Government of Canada

First Major Event

World Cup Pre-Olympic Competition – Six World Records Set

The first weekend of December in 1987 was an historic one for the newly opened Olympic Oval.

Under the leadership of Olympic speed skating committee chairman Klaas Schipper and the Olympiques Calgary Olympics '88 (OCO '88) volunteers, a world cup was held as the Olympic test event to ensure the facility and most importantly the ice were ready. Under ideal high-altitude conditions, without temperature fluctuations, snow, and dust common to outdoor facilities, the Olympic Oval gave skaters and on-lookers a first glimpse of what was to come. Six world records were set right out of the gate. After the event, many attributed the success to "beginners luck". Over the next quarter century, the Oval would see no less than 258 long track records and 30 short track world records smashed under its roof.

Fun Fact

The first man to set a world record at the Olympic Oval was Geir Karlstad of Norway, with a time of 6.43.59 in the 5000-metre distance on December 4, 1987. A day later, Gabi Zange was the first woman to achieve this feat, with a world record time of 4.16.76 in the women's 3000-metre race. Both records were set at the pre-Olympic world cup event, the first competition at the newly built Olympic Oval.

Alberta '88 Celebrity Gala

December 12, 1987 · Shortly after the pre-Olympic speed skating event, the Olympic Oval hosted a celebrity gala as part of an all-expense paid ski weekend and Olympic preview at Mount Allan. The event was sponsored by the Alberta Tourism Department and offered Albertans a once-in-a-lifetime chance to mingle with the stars at $135 per ticket. Proceeds from the gala were to be split between Canadian and U.S. national ski teams.

About three dozen Hollywood celebrities and sports stars came out for the event, including Eva Gabor, I Dream of Jeannie's Barbara Eden, Marlee Matlin, Superman Christopher Reeve, Dan Fogelberg, Rita Coolidge, Brooke Shields and Roger Moore. The stars signed autographs and posed for photos throughout the night. Members of the Canadian speed skating team presented a demonstration of the sport as part of the event.

Art at the Oval

The Government of Canada allocated $400,000 of the $39.9-million budget to build the Olympic Oval art collection. The artwork at the facility acknowledges the deep connections between artists and athletes, and the idea that sport and art are both fundamental forms of expression of the human spirit.

◄ The Spire (1988)

At the north entrance of the Olympic Oval visitors are greeted by The Spire, a large red sculpture created by Calgarian Charles Boyce. The piece is intended to depict a 'progression of human movement,' representing crawling, walking, running, jumping, and flying. In homage to 1988 Olympics it stands 19.88 metres high. The Spire is a somewhat contentious work, often leaving passersby wondering about the artist's intention and vision. In the early years of the Oval's construction, people thought it might be an extension of the duct work for the building or part of the roof. It is now affectionately known, especially in the University of Calgary community, as "the paper-clip".

▲ Brothers of the Wind (1925)

This bronze frieze by well-known Canadian artist Robert Tait McKenzie was completed in 1925 and purchased for the Oval for $75,000. A long-time supporter and spectator at the Olympic Games, McKenzie often participated as an exhibitor during Olympic competitions for fine arts. The Brothers of the Wind is one of McKenzie's finest and largest works. The sculpture is located in the main stairwell in the lobby of the Olympic Oval, which was built specifically to allow the sculpture to recede into the overhang. It depicts eight speed skaters in competition. This glorious piece was replicated in a ceremonial ring which is presented to athletes who set world records in the building. The ring was conceived as a unique, iconic gift from the Olympic Oval to athletes in recognition of their world record achievements.

Olympic Torch and Miners Lamp (1988) ▶

The torch for the 1988 Winter Olympic Games is made of Canadian maple and aluminum, and mirrors the shape of the Calgary Tower. Pictograms of Olympic winter sports are etched into the handle and it is inscribed on the bottom with the Olympic motto, Citius Altius Fortius – faster, higher, stronger. The Miner's Lamp accompanying the torch was used to transport and re-light the flame during the cross-Canada relay. The relay, themed "Share the Flame", was one of the longest in Olympic history, covering a distance of about 18,000 kilometres across Canada.

The Heroic Entrance (1987) ▼

On the upper floor of the Olympic Oval, these marmoleum tiles signal the entrance to the viewing deck. The tiles are a permanent site-specific installation by highly acclaimed Toronto (American-born) artist Barbara Astman. Astman has been commissioned for public art projects since the mid-80s. This floor installation was one of the first public commissions of her career.

▲ Le Patineur de Vitesse 84 (1987)

Le Patineur de Vitesse '84, by Quebec sculptor Germain Bergeron, is located on the south patio of the Olympic Oval. The piece echoes the artist's other stylistic sculptural work and is made of recycled metal. It was created in honour of Canadian speed skater Gaétan Boucher, and reflects the high level of performance fostered at the Oval, as well as Gaétan's achievement of four medals over two Olympics.

▲ The Athlete (1903)

The Athlete is one of two pieces (the other is The Brothers of the Wind) sculpted by Robert Tait McKenzie. The piece is a composite of average body measurements of 400 Harvard men, eventually distilled into the proportions of the 50 strongest of these men over a period of eight years.

◀ The Speed Skater (1984)

This bronze sculpture by John Weaver was part of a fundraising campaign in Calgary's bid to host the 1988 Winter Olympics. The statue is one of only five sculptures in Weaver's series designed to portray Olympic winter athletes and is currently on permanent display in the Oval lobby. Weaver was the resident sculptor at Alberta's provincial museum in the 1980s and is most famous for creating the statue of Wayne Gretzky (1989) outside Rexall Place in Edmonton.

▲ Pagoglyphs (Marks on Ice) (1987)

Brian Baxter of Vancouver designed two stained glass windows (one depicted above) for each of the main entrances to the Oval. Made with a mixture of manufactured and hand blown glass, prisms and mirrors, the pieces create the effect of skate marks on ice. The windows were commissioned at a total cost of $40,000.

"We'll probably break all the world records here…We've had a great response from all the skaters who have trained here so far – the Canadians, the Americans, the Germans and the Austrians. They all love it because the ice is so fast…"

– Cathy Priestner Allinger

"Best Ever Games"

XV Olympic Winter Games, Calgary, Canada – February 13-28, 1988

The Olympic flame arrived in Calgary on February 13, 1988 after an 88-day cross country odyssey, signaling the start of the 1988 Winter Olympic Games.

88 Olympic Oval general manager and 1976 long track speed skating Olympic silver medallist Cathy Priestner Allinger, along with ski racer, two-time Olympian and leader of the "Crazy Canucks" Ken Read, carried the torch into a jam-packed McMahon Stadium.

Along the way they stopped to greet Rick Hansen, who had just completed his Man in Motion World Tour and then to the surprise of the world handed the flame to 12-year-old Robyn Perry to light the cauldron. Perry represented the future potential of the world's youth. The next day, and throughout the Games, Priestner Allinger and the Olympic Oval would see triumph, adversity and the beginning of a legacy that would last well beyond the Olympic Games.

The new indoor speed skating venue was the one to watch in 1988. Expectations for the Olympic Oval were set in 1987 when six world records fell. The world anticipated stellar performances at the Olympic Games because of the controlled conditions and fast ice. The Oval did not disappoint.

Triumph and Adversity

During the competition, 119 skaters from 19 countries took to the ice at the Olympic Oval. In total, eight world records were set at the Olympic Oval during the Games.

Dutch speed skating sensation Yvonne van Gennip won gold and smashed both the 3000-metre and 5000-metre women's records and added a third gold medal in the 1500-metre event. The 5000-metre race for the women was the first ever in a Winter Olympic Games. Her three golds were the most medals won by a female speed skater since Lydia Skoblikova of the Soviet Union won four at the 1964 Winter Games in Innsbruck, Austria. As the 15 days came to a close, Yvonne would be honoured as the single most decorated athlete of the Games.

There were other triumphs too. American Bonnie Blair set the world record in the 500-metre race. Uwe-Jens Mey and Andre Hoffman (GDR), Tomas Gustafson (SWE) and Yong-Hun Song (PRK) also set world records during the 1988 Games.

Gaétan Boucher

Crowds at the '88 Games were hoping for a comeback for Boucher. At the time, he was Canada's most revered and famous speed skater and fans were behind him, crossing their fingers that he would win a medal in his home country. He was Canada's most decorated winter Olympian. He represented success in speed skating and in a wider sense successes in sport in the international arena.

Coming into the Games, Boucher desperately wanted a medal to add to the three he'd earned in Sarajevo in 1984 and the one from Lake Placid in 1980. This would be his last Olympics and he wanted to go out on a high. Unfortunately, he was dealing with an ankle injury that ultimately affected his technique and speed. This led to a 14th place finish in the 500-metre race and a 5th place in the 1000-metre event, his last race of the Games. He didn't win a medal, but the crowd of 4,500 at the Olympic Oval gave him a standing ovation after his last race. They were moved by his courage and determination and wanted to acknowledge his contribution to Canadian sport.

Gaétan inspired, and continues to inspire, speed skaters in Canada and the world over. It was fitting that he finished his career at the Olympic Oval, an inspirational venue that would continue to build on the foundation he established.

Dan Jansen

He was expected to medal. Possibly break a world record. But for American speed skater Dan Jansen, 1988 was rife with sadness. On the same day East German skater Uwe-Jens Mey set the men's world record in the 500-metre, Dan Jansen awoke to a phone call with the news that his 27 year-old sister Jane had died from leukemia. The capacity crowd looked on and all hearts were with him as the news of his sister's death echoed in the arena. It was a difficult race. Jansen committed a false start and was then eliminated after he fell on the first corner. "I did my best. I know Jane would have wanted that," he said afterwards. "Maybe it just wasn't meant to be."

It was an emotional blow to the young skater to be sure, but it was buffered by the love and support extended to him by the crowd and his friends and family at the Oval. Jansen's family and good friend Bonnie Blair were there for support.

Long Track Canadian Olympic Team, 1988 Calgary Games

- Gaétan Boucher
- Chantal Côté
- Gordon Goplen
- Kathy Gordon
- Natalie Grenier
- Gregor Jelonek
- Benoit Lamarche
- Marie-Pierre Lamarche
- Ariane Loignon
- Caroline Maheux
- Jean Pichette
- Shelley Rhead-Skarvan
- Guy Thibault
- Marcel Tremblay
- Robert Tremblay
- Daniel Turcotte

Go to the Start

"There has been resistance from traditionalists in the past. But now a lot of them realize that this is a coming sport."
– Alan Jones, vice-president of the Canadian Amateur Speed Skating Association, 1988

Short Track Canadian Olympic Team, 1988 Calgary Games

- Susan Auch
- Sylvie Daigle
- Michel Daignault
- Eden Donatelli
- Robert Dubreuil
- Louis Genier
- Nathalie Lambert
- Marye Perreault
- Mario Vincent

88 A short track milestone occurred in 1988 when the sport made its Olympic debut as a demonstration event at the Calgary Winter Olympic Games. The event was held at Max Bell Arena.

Organizers hoped that short track would go on to become an official medal sport at the next Winter Games at Albertville, France, in 1992 – which it did. In Calgary, events were held for both women and men in the 500-metre, 1000-metre, 1500-metre, 3000-metre and the relay events (3000-metre for women, 5000-metre for men). Canada took home a total of ten medals, the most medals by any country in the demonstration event. Skaters from The Netherlands picked up nine and Japan and China claimed three each. Sylvie Daigle was the stand-out Canadian winning silver in the women's 1000 metres, gold in the women's 1500 metres and silver in the women's 3000 metres. Future long track Canadian speed skater and two-time Olympic medallist Susan Auch also competed in her first Olympics at this short track event.

Fun Fact

Students from the U of C generously offered their residences to thousands of athletes as Kananaskis, Rundle, Castle, Norquay and Brewster halls became the Athlete's Village for the '88 Games. Glacier and Olympus halls were newly constructed to house additional athletes. The village was bustling with activity, including hosting concerts by music stars such as Bryan Adams and K.D. Lang.

Starting a Family

The 1988 Winter Games were an important milestone for the Olympic Oval not just for the competition results, but also because the venue brought an extended family to the building that would last a lifetime.

88 The first three years at the Oval after the 1988 Olympics set a standard of excellence for years to come, with a number of high profile speed skating competitions, sports events and community events being held at the facility. Local, national, and international athletes arrived in Calgary and numerous community organizations took advantage of the space and amenities at the new venue (and still do to this day).

The Oval also became home to Canadian and American athletes who trained at the facility before and after the Games. For those already in the speed skating world, the Oval was instantly recognized as a special place. For those who didn't know the sport, the Oval showcased speed skating in an unprecedented way, introducing them to the power, athleticism and head-to-head excitement of long track competition.

Most importantly, the Olympic Oval allowed Canadian athletes to train and develop on home soil. Canadian speed skaters, prior to the construction of the Oval, left the country for extended periods to train. They would leave in September, return home in December for Canadian trials and then leave again to train and race abroad from January through March. This was very difficult for the skaters, coaches and their families. The advent of the Oval signaled the acceleration of the development of the national long track team, who (as predicted by general manager Cathy Priestner Allinger) would go on to dominate the speed skating world within the decade. The Oval became their home ice and gave them access to year-round training.

Finally, the local community instantly saw the impact of having the Games in their backyard. There was an influx of activity around the Oval from national and international athletes, who were seen running, cycling and training in the neighbourhood. The Games also prompted Calgarians (and Canadians) to get fit and inspired some to begin Olympic journeys of their own.

Welcomed with Open Arms

American Dan Jansen and Canadian speed skater Gregor Jelonek recall how special the Games were, and tell stories of the Adopt-a-Parent program that placed the families of competing athletes with local Calgarians for home-stay accommodation during the Games. During the Olympics, Dan's family stayed with a special woman by the name of Bea Cochrane, who lived close to the Oval. After 1988, Dan stayed there while training in Calgary. Many other athletes had similar experiences with their Olympic families, a testament to the generosity of the people of Calgary and area.

Gregor Jelonek

Gregor Jelonek was a member of the Canadian national long track team from 1987 to 1992, and competed in the 1988 Calgary Winter Olympics. He was also on the first long track team to train at the new indoor Olympic Oval when it first opened. Gregor has stayed connected to the facility over the last 25 years, first as an athlete and then as a coach. He was part of the Canadian long track coaching team for both the 2006 Torino Winter Games and 2010 Vancouver Winter Olympic Games. He was named SSC's Coach of the Year in 2000, 2012 and 2013.

A Facility Becomes a Home

1988 Legacy Venue, not a White Elephant

After the 1988 Winter Olympics, the futures of the facilities built for the Games were in question. Calgary was now home to one of only three indoor speed skating ovals in the world, Canada's only bobsled and luge runs, two regulation-size ski jumps and a $100-million ice arena (the Olympic Saddledome). Outside city limits there were other venues too—the Canmore Nordic Centre and Nakiska ski area. The bill for the facilities totaled approximately $400-million.

In the community there was talk of the legacy being unsustainable. Could these venues be viable as future training and competition sites? Would athletes be able to afford to train at them long-term? The Olympic Oval was one venue that put these fears to rest.

Shortly after the Games the Canadian long track team moved to Calgary to take advantage of the fast ice and year round training. Europeans and Americans followed. These votes of confidence meant the Oval would last.

The three years following the Winter Olympic Games were critical for the Oval. A standard of excellence had to be established for the venue to survive, and it was. The fast ice continued to shine. Mark Messer, Cam McLeod and the Oval ice technicians worked tirelessly to maintain an ice surface that was unmatched.

Cathy Priestner Allinger remained at the helm as general manager and during her tenure she launched the Oval on an upward trajectory. She anticipated that it would take 10 years for Canadian speed skaters to dominate the sport. She branded the facility as the best; she hired Jacques Thibault to oversee the technical programs; she approached the provinces for financial support to send their skaters to the Oval to train with the best coaches; she went head-to-head with CODA for programming funds; and she nurtured partnerships with athletics, cycling, and eventually women's hockey and welcomed other high performance sports into the building.

Priestner Allinger was the person behind many firsts, including the initiative for summer ice at the Oval. On-ice training in the summer was a hugely innovative idea and created a big change in the sport of speed skating. The plan was proposed to the U of C and they gave the Oval permission to implement summer training as a test project for two years, thinking it wouldn't last. There were many who still envisioned the Olympic Oval as a multi-use facility—a skating rink in the winter and a field house in the summer.

Word of summer ice at the Oval spread and European skaters started to arrive in Calgary to use it. The Canadians did not embrace the idea of incorporating summer ice into their training programs until the mid-90s. They feared burnout from training on ice year round and were resistant to changes in their routine. But the popularity of summer training and development camps with the international skaters guaranteed the year-round training program would stay beyond the two-year trial period.

Finally, Priestner Allinger established a culture of teamwork, believing that a team approach from administration, coaches and athletes was the only way to nurture excellence. At the time this was innovative and people questioned her approach.

From 1989 to 1992 the groundwork for the next 25 years was established. These years opened the flood gates for the Oval to become the crown jewel of the speed skating world, "Canada's Medal Factory", and the place where ordinary people achieve extraordinary things.

Ollie is Unveiled

In 1989 the Oval mascot, Ollie the Penguin, was introduced to the world.

89

His unveiling took place twice: once on September 15 during a lunchtime public skating session, along with the University of Calgary mascot Dexter the Dinosaur, and again on October 29 at the Olympic Oval Halloween party.

The initial concept for Ollie came from 11th grade part-time Oval staff member Kristy (Elisha) Hawrys. He was developed into a mascot by Glenn Street, owner of local Calgary props company Street Characters. His full name at his inception was Oil Can Ollie, but he was officially named Ollie.

The new mascot had a very involved background story, which served to make him a true character. It was said he came to the Olympic Oval after hearing about the 1988 Olympic Winter Games and he swam all the way from Antarctica to see it. Because the distance was so great, it took him a year to reach his destination. When he finally arrived, like so many others, Ollie knew he was home!

Ollie has undergone several makeovers through the years, but he still lives at the Oval year round. He makes appearances during public skating, special events and ventures out into the community on a regular basis sharing his love of skating and the Olympic Oval, his adopted home.

Screen Time

A number of commercials, television programs and movies have been shot at the Olympic Oval. Watch these reels closely to see members of the Oval family featured as stars or extras.

Television & Commercials

1994 • Skippy Peanut Butter commercial with Bonnie Blair.

1998 • General Motors "Spirit of Sport" commercial.

2005 • Bridgestone Blizzack Tire "Need New Tires" commercial featuring Mario Andretti filmed at the Olympic Oval and tire testing performed on Oval ice.

2006 • Rick Mercer Report – Rick Mercer trains to develop "speed skater thighs" with long track national team member Shannon Rempel.

2009 • Samsung MTS commercial with Cindy Klassen.

2010 • Rick Mercer Report – Rick Mercer visits the Olympic Oval with Canadian Olympic gymnast Kyle Shewflet and CEO of Own the Podium Roger Jackson.

2010 • Vancouver 2010 "Do You Believe" commercials.

2010 • CTV Olympic Coverage – Olympic figure skaters Jamie Salé and David Pelletier try out speed skating with Olympian Denny Morrison and coach Marcel Lacroix.

2012 • Calgary 2012 Artist-in-Residence Films – The Artist in Residency (AiR) Program was designed to explore the Calgary 2012 themes of Looking Back, Calgary Now and Looking Forward and connect artists and historians with other aspects of Calgary's diverse identity.

The Olympic Oval's Calgary 2012 AIR, Ramin Eshraghi-Yazdi celebrated our 25th anniversary season filming and producing six short films that were screened at the Oval during the 25th Anniversary celebrations and released worldwide, one at a time, weekly on YouTube.

Films

1993 – Cool Runnings

Cool Runnings was shot in and around Calgary, with some of the scenes shot inside the Olympic Oval. It was very loosely based on the adventures of the Jamaican national bobsled team at the 1988 Olympics.

2002 – Rollerball

Rollerball was shot in Montreal and around southern Alberta. Chris Klein, one of the film's stars, worked with the Oval Program speed skating coaches to hone his skating technique.

Setting the Standard

Back together

Calgary Olympic committee speed skating chairman Klaas Schipper brought together a group of volunteers to organize the speed skating events, including the 1987 pre-Olympic event and the 1988 Olympic Winter Games. Twenty-five years later, many of the original volunteers are still actively involved and continue to organize competitions on behalf of Speed Skating Canada. Over the years, these volunteers have helped stage more than 50 national and international competitions held at the Olympic Oval. Their excellence is recognized by many, including the International Skating Union.

The first international event after the Olympics was a two-day ladies world cup event, held February 11-12, 1989. Women from 10 countries competed, including 1988 Olympic medal winners Christina Rothenburger (GDR) and Bonnie Blair (USA).

Rothenburger placed first and Blair finished second in the 500-metre and the 1000-metre events respectively.

Immediately following this event, the Canadian Amateur Speed Skating

Association was awarded three additional International Skating Union (ISU) competitions to take place at the Olympic Oval, including: the World Championships All-Round for Women (Feb. 9-10, 1990), the World Junior Championships (Mar. 1-3, 1991) and the World Championships All-Round for Men (Mar. 21-22, 1992). The success of the Olympics and the world records established under the near-perfect conditions at the venue helped the effort to bring the ISU events to Calgary.

Several Canadian Championships, national and international competitions were also held during this period. A total of 11 world records were set between 1989 and 1992.

Spirit of '88 Best Ever Volunteers Continue to Support Speed Skating

After the 1988 Winter Olympic Games Roger Jackson and the 1988 Organizing Committee volunteers reunited to bring events to the facility, drawing people back to experience the thrill of competition and world records. These speed skating enthusiasts' continued to dedicate their time and energy to events at the Olympic Oval. Under the name Olympic Oval Organizing Committee

or OOOC (now the Organizing Committee Calgary) this group has hosted over 50 speed skating competitions at the venue since 1988. Many of the original members of this group are still on the committee today. This is a testament to the human legacy of volunteer spirit that has remained since the Winter Olympic Games.

The committee has had three chairpersons over its 25-year history – Klaas Schipper, Roger Jackson and Alice Humeny.

Fun Facts

- It takes 200-250 volunteers to run a World Championship competition.

- There are about 20 volunteers who have been involved with the Calgary Organizing Committee since 1988.

- The largest world cup event held at the Oval was in December 2009, prior to the Vancouver Winter Olympics. A record number of countries (33) and a record number of skaters (296) participated. A total of 232 volunteers put in 4,444 hours of work. During the three-day event, skaters consumed over 2,000 bananas!

- The 2009 event earned the nickname "World Record World Cup". Number of hotel room nights: 1,991. Number of fans attending: 3,150 + 977 school children on Friday. Number of doping control tests: 27. Number of accreditation cards issued: 1,135. Number of airport transfers: 812

- Economic impact of 2011 World Sprint Championships in the Calgary community: 1120 hotel rooms for athletes, officials and delegates; 30 international media attending; 300 international fans (mostly from The Netherlands); estimated $2-million of economic activity generated.

- The World Sprint Championships at the Oval in January 2003 had a sell-out crowd of 4,650 spectators as Canadians competed at home.

- The 2011 Essent ISU World All-Round Speed Skating Championships draw was held at the newly opened Canada Sports Hall of Fame.

Events

International Competitions coordinated by the Calgary Organizing Committee on behalf of Speed Skating Canada

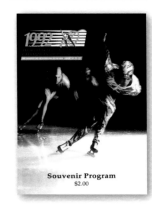

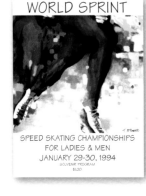

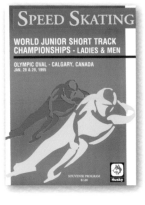

1988
- CanAm Meet (Canada vs. USA)

1989
- CanAm Meet
- World Cup for Ladies

1990
- CanAm Meet
- World Speed Skating Championship for Ladies
- World Cup for Ladies and Men

1991
- North American Long Track Championships
- World Junior Speed Skating Championships for Ladies and Men

1992
- Olympic Team Trials
- World Speed Skating Championship for Men

1993
- International Standards Competition
- Primary Olympic Trials

1994
- Final Olympic Trials
- World Sprint Speed Skating Championships for Ladies and Men
- CODA Invitational Short Track Competition

1995
- World Junior Short Track Championships for Ladies and Men
- World Cup for Ladies and Men – Sprints

1996
- World Junior Championships for Ladies and Men
- World Cup for Ladies and Men – All distances

1997
- World Cup for Ladies and Men – Sprints (January)
- Junior Country Match
- World Cup for Ladies and Men – Sprints (November)

1998
- World Speed Skating Single Distance Championships for Ladies and Men

1999
- World Sprint Speed Skating Championships for Ladies and Men

2000
- Essent ISU World Cup Speed Skating

2001
- Essent ISU World Cup Speed Skating (March)
- Essent ISU World Cup Speed Skating (December)

2003
- World Sprint Speed Skating Championships (January)
- Essent ISU World Cup Speed Skating (December)

2005
- Essent ISU World Cup Speed Skating (January)
- Essent ISU World Cup Speed Skating (November)

2006
- ISU World All-Round Speed Skating Championships (March)

2007
- Essent ISU World Cup Speed Skating (March)
- Essent ISU World Cup Speed Skating (November)

2009
- Essent ISU World Cup Speed Skating (December)

2011
- Essent ISU World All-Round Speed Skating Championships (February)

2012
- Essent ISU World Sprint Speed Skating Championships (January)

2013
- Essent ISU World Cup Speed Skating (January)

Awarded

2013
- Essent ISU World Cup Speed Skating (November)

2015
- World All-Round Speed Skating Championships

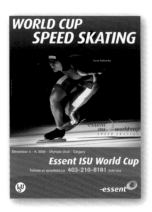

The Fastest Ice in the World™

In speed skating and other ice sports there is no question that the skating surface can be a game-changer.

Fast ice often provides an extra edge for an athlete to break a record, improve a performance or set a personal best. Chief ice-maker Mark Messer and the ice technicians at the Olympic Oval work tirelessly to create and maintain The Fastest Ice in the World™.

Ice-making in the building is both an art and a science. Calgary's altitude and unique Chinook weather conditions are considerations during the process. The humidity in the building and the number of spectators at any given competition are also part of the equation. The four key components in making great ice are: water, temperature, hardness and thickness. Different ice conditions are required for long track, short track, hockey and figure skating.

Figure skating ice is thicker and softer than hockey ice, allowing skaters to dig in and carve. In speed skating, long track ice is dense and hard for increased glide, whereas short track ice is softer for extra grip. At the Olympic Oval, the ice is made directly on the concrete and painted according to the needs of the sport. Temperatures on the three ice surfaces are independently controlled and range from -2 to -9 degrees Celsius.

Deionized water is necessary to make speed skating ice as it reduces impurities and reduces friction with the skater's blade. This allows for the purest most perfect ice surface possible. The colder and purer the ice, the longer the glide for the skater and the less energy expended. Ice impurities can also dull skates making a significant difference in lap times and performance.

The Olympic Oval uses two ice-resurfacing machines to remove dirt and imperfections that occur over the course of a day. One of the machines is one and a half times larger than standard size and is used to efficiently clean the large surface of the 400-metre oval track.

In total, over 50,000 personal-best times, 258 long track world records and 30 short track world records have been set at the Olympic Oval over the past 25 years. These stunning statistics are in no small part due to the dedication of the ice technicians working closely with the coaches and athletes to create the best quality skating surface, which is inarguably The Fastest Ice in the World™.

Fun Fact

The Fastest Ice in the World™ was trademarked in 2001.

Six Step Ice-Making Process

1 The pad is cooled to about -7°C by sending salt water through the pipes embedded in the concrete.

2 Three light coats of demineralized water are sprayed on the pad, freezing instantly.

3 Three passes of white spray paint are applied, also freezing immediately.

4 Water is sprayed to seal the paint and prevent it from migrating to the surface.

5 Dots, lines and logos are applied to indicate start lines and lanes.

6 The entire pad is flooded to 2.5 cm thick, and ice temperature is maintained between -4°C and -10°C.

Calgary Facts

- Altitude: 1,079 m
- Oval altitude: 1,105.42 m at ice level
- Average temperature: high 11°C, low -2°C
- Monthly possible temperature fluctuation: 27°C
- Warmest average high temperature: 24°C (75°F) in July
- Coolest average low temperature: -16°C (3°F) in January
- Mean relative humidity: yearly, 57.0% and monthly, ranges from 45% in May to 70% in November and December

Indoor Ovals Around the World

As the first covered speed skating oval in North America used for an Olympic Games, the Calgary facility, along with the University of Calgary, has provided guidance to many delegations embarking on the potential design and construction of their own legacy speed skating facilities.

Indoor Oval Timeline Selection

1985 • November 17 – The first indoor artificial speed skating oval built, Sportforum Hohenschönhausen, Berlin, Germany. Seating capacity 4,695.

1986 • November – Thialf indoor oval in Heerenveen, Netherlands opens. The arena has a capacity of 12,500.

1987 • First North American artificial speed skating oval completed, Olympic Oval, Calgary, Canada. Grand opening September 27, 1987. In 1988, is the first indoor oval used for the Winter Olympic Games. Since the 1994 Winter Olympics in Lillehammer all speed skating competitions have been held indoors.

1992 • Hamar Olympic Hall or Vikingskipet ("The Viking Ship") opens in December 1992. Built for the 1994 Winter Olympics in Lillehammer, Norway.

1993 • The Pettit National Ice Center opens in Milwaukee, Wisconsin on January 1, 1993. Becomes home to the U.S. national speed skating team.

1996 • M-Wave opens in Nagano, Japan. The arena has a capacity of 10,000. Host of speed skating events for the 1998 Winter Olympics.

2001 • Utah Olympic Oval completed. Hosts speed skating events for the 2002 Winter Olympics in Salt Lake City, Utah.

2005 • Torino Oval Lingotto built for use at the 2006 Torino Winter Olympics. Capacity: 8,500 spectators.

2007 • Fosenhallen in Bjugn, Norway opens in September 2007. A multi-use facility consisting of a speed skating rink, ice hockey rink, curling rink and football field.

2008 • The Richmond Olympic Oval completed. Was the venue for speed skating events for the 2010 Vancouver Winter Olympics. The Richmond Olympic venue was converted to a recreational centre after the 2010 Games.

2009 • Fort St. John Oval, British Columbia, Canada opens. Includes walking track and two hockey rinks plus elevated 400-metre oval on second level.

2010 • Minsk-Arena Complex opens in Minsk, Belarus. Includes a multi-sport and entertainment arena with seating for 15,000 people, a velodrome with seating for 2,000, and an ice skating oval seating 3,000 people.

2010 • Sørmarka Arena Stavanger, Norway opens. Seats 4,000 people.

2012 • The Adler Arena Skating Center, an 8,000-seat multi-purpose arena opens in Sochi, Russia. Host to speed skating events for the 2014 Winter Olympic Games.

There are currently 29 sheltered ovals around the world:

- The Netherlands.............................5
- Russia 5
- Norway 4
- Canada..3
- Germany...3
- China...2
- Japan...2
- Belarus 1
- Italy...1
- Kazakhstan....................................1
- Korea...1
- Sweden...1

Brothers of the Wind

The Brothers of the Wind world record ring is modeled after the bronze frieze by Robert Tait McKenzie that is mounted in the Olympic Oval stairwell to the upstairs viewing deck.

The ring is presented to skaters who set world records at ISU sanctioned speed skating competitions. Those awarded the ring are part of a special brotherhood/sisterhood of athletes who are connected to the Oval and to each other, no matter where they are.

The first ring was presented in the 1990-1991 season. This was the beginning of a tradition that continues to this day. Skaters who set multiple world records have the choice of receiving another ring or adding a diamond to their existing ring each time they break a world record at the Olympic Oval. Senior skaters are awarded a gold ring, while junior skaters are given a silver ring for world record achievements.

Top 10 Most Decorated Olympic Oval Brothers of the Wind World Record Holders

- 22   Jeremy Wotherspoon, CAN
- 11   Catriona Le May Doan, CAN
- 9   Cindy Klassen, CAN
- 8   Anni Friesinger, GER
- 7   Ireen Wüst, NED
- 6   Bonnie Blair, USA
- 5   Jae-Bong Choi, KOR
- 5   Dan Jansen, USA
- 5   Chris Witty, USA
- 5   Falko Zandstra. NED

Fun Fact

Catriona Le May Doan (CAN) set 11 world records at the Oval (13 in total) and has received five Brothers of the Wind rings. Catriona has one ring set with four diamonds. She gave other rings to: her husband Bart, her mother, her coach in 1998 Derrick Auch, and her exercise physiologist at the U of C human performance lab Dr. Dave Smith. Her two remaining rings will be given to her children.

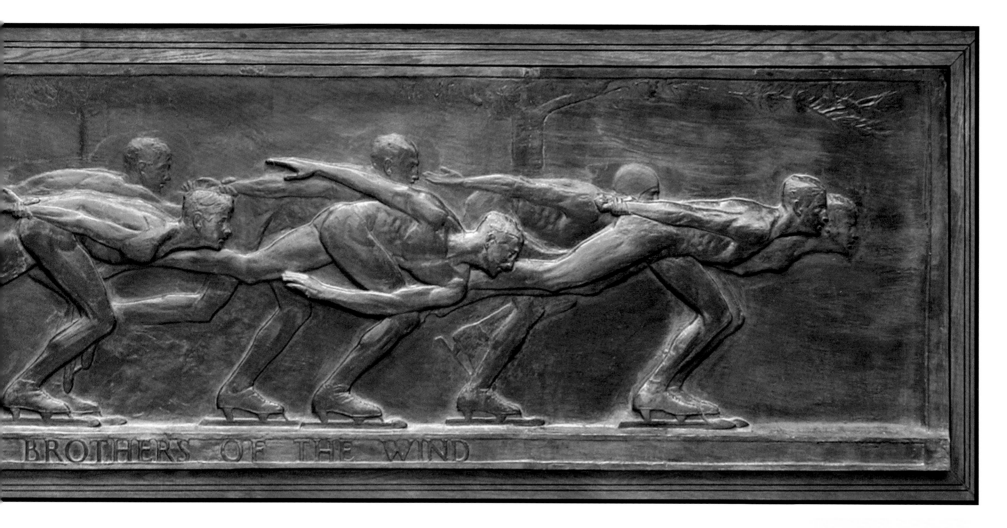

BROTHERS OF THE WIND

Brothers of the Wind Significant Awards

Brothers of the Wind Significant Awards are given to recognize excellence in other areas:
• In the early years, a Brothers of the Wind pin was given to skaters who set a country record. Senior skaters received a gold pin and junior skaters were awarded a silver pin. This award was reinstated for the 25th anniversary celebration at the 2013 Oval Finale.

Oval Staff Brothers of the Wind Service Awards

• 10 years of service: men receive a Brothers of the Wind tie clip, women receive a Brothers of the Wind pendant necklace.
• 15 years of service: framed Brothers of the Wind print.
• 20 years of service: men receive a ring replicating the Olympic Oval roof, while women receive a Brothers of the Wind bracelet.

Fun Fact

At the 1997 Oval Finale a limited edition Brothers of the Wind print was provided as the Finale personal best gift.

1992

"There's nothing like it anywhere."

– Bonnie Blair

Skate to Albertville

XVI Olympic Winter Games, Albertville, France – February 8-23, 1992

The 1992 Winter Olympic Games in Albertville were the first Winter Olympics since Calgary in 1988. They were notable for speed skating in that full medal status was granted to short track.

Canada captured three short track medals in Albertville. The silver medal winning men's 5000-metre relay included Mark Lackie, who shortly following Albertville would arrive at the Oval as one of the first skaters in the Oval high performance short track program.

On an outdoor oval, our American "cousin" who trained at the Calgary Oval, Bonnie Blair, brought home another 500-metre gold medal. Her emotional win at the 1988 Olympics was a highlight of those Games. Although the Canadian long track team did not medal at these Games, Albertville was the first Olympics where the skaters who trained at the Oval gave the world a glimpse of what was to come.

The Oval Celebrates the Albertville Winter Games

Starting in January of 1992 the Olympic Oval held a public event for the community to celebrate the Olympics and get people into the spirit for the upcoming Albertville Games. The event was called "Skate to Albertville" and allowed participants to track their kilometers on the speed skating track, with the goal to log the distance from Calgary to Albertville – a total of 7,851 kilometers.

Each participant purchased a 20-pass for public skating at a reduced rate and they were given until February 7, 1992 to reach the goal. Prizes were drawn to award those who completed the challenge, and all finishers had their names placed on a temporary Olympic Wall of Fame.

Oval Trained Athletes in Albertville

- **Speed Skating:** Susan Auch, Robert Dubreuil, Sean Ireland, Patrick Kelly, Catriona Le May Doan, Neal Marshall, Shelley Rhead-Skarvan, John Kevin Scott, Guy Thibault

- **Short Track:** Mark Lackie

Along with these Canadian Olympians many athletes, coaches and support staff called the Oval home prior to participating in these Olympics.

Oval Program Takes Off

The Olympic Oval is arguably the hub of long track speed skating in Canada and a force in the international speed skating community worldwide.

The Olympic Oval High Performance program in long track started shortly after the 1988 Calgary Winter Olympics when it was apparent the skaters, both from Canada and abroad, needed a place to train year-round. At the time, the Oval was the only covered speed skating oval in North America, and one of a few in the world.

The Oval was, from the very beginning, an international training facility, hosting athletes from Argentina, Austria, Belarus, Columbia, China, Greece, Japan, Kazakhstan, Korea, Latvia, The Netherlands, New Zealand, Sweden, Switzerland, Ukraine, and the United States (among others). These athletes came to Canada for the legendary fast ice, the desirable indoor conditions, and the technical knowledge at the facility. The Oval Program was built on the passion and expertise of the people involved – athletes, coaches, friends, family and community. It was a program that built champions and inspired a culture of excellence.

As the long track programs progressed, the Oval produced a long line of world cup, World Championship and Olympic medallists. Talented athletes were given a chance to achieve their best performances and train under coaches who inspired them to win. The training model is based on a team approach, learning from other sport disciplines, and hard work.

The success of programs at the Olympic Oval is largely because of the attitude of the athletes, coaches and support staff. Throughout the years the facility developed a culture of excellence and the basic belief that it was a place where champions are built. The programs were seen as the core and the heart of the Oval. Everything revolved around working to create champions.

Skaters from a high performance level advance through the programs and develop into competitive elite athletes. Young skaters are exposed to the high performance environment early on, training alongside elite senior national team athletes, and are inspired to achieve their dreams.

The Olympic Oval's high performance programs have grown to training more than 150 athletes per year (ranging from provincial team to national team) and employing more than 10 speed skating coaches.

Short Track Comes to the Oval

The "Dirty Dozen"

First high performance short track athletes training at the Olympic Oval

- Guy Bushell, Great Britain
- Derrick Campbell, ONT
- Heather Gallagher, ONT
- Rebecca "Becky" Hamilton, ONT
- Shawn Holman, ONT
- Mark Lackie, NB
- Nadine Landry, QUE
- Tony Main, ONT
- John Munroe, AB
- Trish Proctor, MAN
- Andrew Quinn, ONT
- Mark Wild, ONT

Short track speed skating was a demonstration sport at the Calgary Winter Olympics in 1988. The short track events during the Games took place at Max Bell arena, as the Olympic Oval focused on the long track events. At the 1992 Winter Olympics in Albertville, France, short track became an official Olympic event and the Canadians brought home three medals from these Games. In August of 1992, the short track program at the Olympic Oval officially started.

After the success of Canadian short track skaters in Albertville, it was identified there was a need for a national short track training centre in western Canada. At the time, the majority of short track athletes came from Quebec and the only national training centre was in Montreal. Jacques Thibault initiated discussions for the Olympic Oval to become the location for this new centre. In June of 1992 the Canadian Amateur Speed Skating Association gave the go ahead for the centre.

Andrew Barron was hired as the first Oval program short track coach. Barron was a national long track team coach. He may not have fit the perceived mold of a short track coach, but he brought a wealth of knowledge and training expertise to the emerging, now Olympic sport. He incorporated new training methods and science for the team by adding multi-disciplinary off-ice body training such as gymnastics, rock climbing and martial arts to the routine. These methods were cutting-edge and extremely innovative for the time.

Derrick Campbell, Shawn Holman and Mark Lackie were three national team short track athletes of a core group of about twelve who moved west to participate. Many of these skaters came to the Oval on blind faith from well-established programs in their home provinces. Marcel Lacroix also headed west from Montreal, joining forces to coach in 1993.

From this small group of dedicated people, the short track program grew. Skaters from all over the world came to the Oval to train and it became the first truly international training centre for short track. Short track athletes could train in the same facility as long track skaters and athletes from other sports. This was influential in that it exposed everyone to new and innovative ideas, allowed cross-pollination between sports and brought people to a new level of excellence.

The program started from nothing, but was successful because of passionate individuals working toward a common goal. The short track program moving to Calgary can partially be attributed to the spike in long track performances of Canadians, per-formances fostered by shared equipment and training knowledge between the short track and long track disciplines. Later, many international athletes would come to train in Calgary to seek out this expertise to stay competitive with the Canadians.

One of the first tangible successes for the program was at a pre-Olympic event in Hamar, Norway in February of 1993. Canadian short track speed skaters raced to a world record in the 3000-metre relay with a time of 4.14.72. Mark Lackie and Derrick Campbell, who were two of the first athletes to join the western Canadian short track program, were members of this team.

In the coming years, the Oval program would nurture athletes to the national team level and gold medal winning performances.

Long Track

Speed skating takes place on a 400-metre track with two racing lanes and an inner warm up lane. The official individual race distances include 500, 1000, 1500, 3000, 5000 (for women) and 10,000 (for men) metres. The Team Pursuit consists of two teams composed of three skaters, racing to be the first team to complete six laps for women and eight laps for men. Standard Olympic style races occur in pairs skating counter clockwise changing lanes every lap on the back straight-away to equalize the distance covered. Skaters race against the clock for the best time in each distance.

Fun Fact

Officials designate athlete lanes with coloured armbands. To remember which athlete started in the inner or outer lane think "apple," red on the outside and white on the inside.

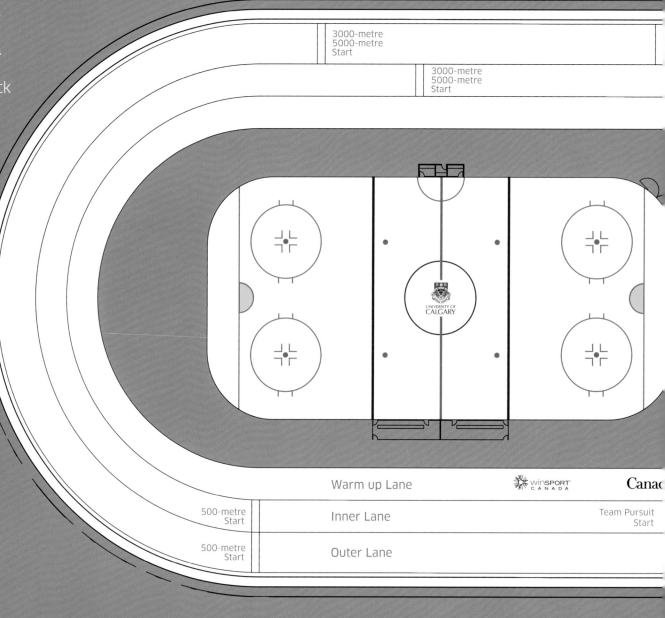

3000-metre
5000-metre
Start

3000-metre
5000-metre
Start

UNIVERSITY OF CALGARY

Warm up Lane

winSPORT
CANADA

Canad

500-metre
Start

Inner Lane

Team Pursuit
Start

500-metre
Start

Outer Lane

Short Track

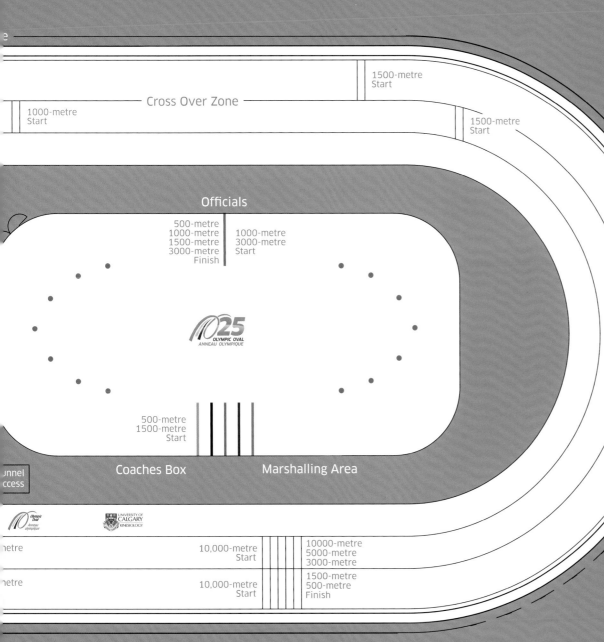

Cross Over Zone

1000-metre
Start

1500-metre
Start

1500-metre
Start

Officials

500-metre
1000-metre
1500-metre
3000-metre
Finish

1000-metre
3000-metre
Start

25
OLYMPIC OVAL
ANNEAU OLYMPIQUE

500-metre
1500-metre
Start

Coaches Box

Marshalling Area

Tunnel
Access

Olympic
Oval
Anneau
olympique

UNIVERSITY OF
CALGARY
KINESIOLOGY

10,000-metre
Start

10000-metre
5000-metre
3000-metre

10,000-metre
Start

1500-metre
500-metre
Finish

Short track speed skating occurs on a 111.12-metre oval track on a rink measuring 60 metres by 30 metres. Corners are tight and race distances include 500, 1000, 1500 and 3000 metres for individual races and relay races of 3000 metres for women and 5000 metres for men. Races are mass start with four to eight skaters on the track at once. Strategy is very important in short track and skaters jostle and maneuver for position during races. The winner of the race is determined by placing at the finish line. Crashes are not uncommon, making it an exciting sport to watch.

International Hockey Rink

The Oval hockey rink follows the International Ice Hockey Federation (IIHF) specifications, of 60 metres × 30 metres with a corner radius of 8.5 metres. The distance from the end boards to the nearest goal line is 4 metres. The distance from each goal line to the nearest blue line is 17 metres.

Gear Guide

The development of indoor long track and short track speed skating training and competing under one roof accelerated the evolution of equipment to achieve faster speeds.

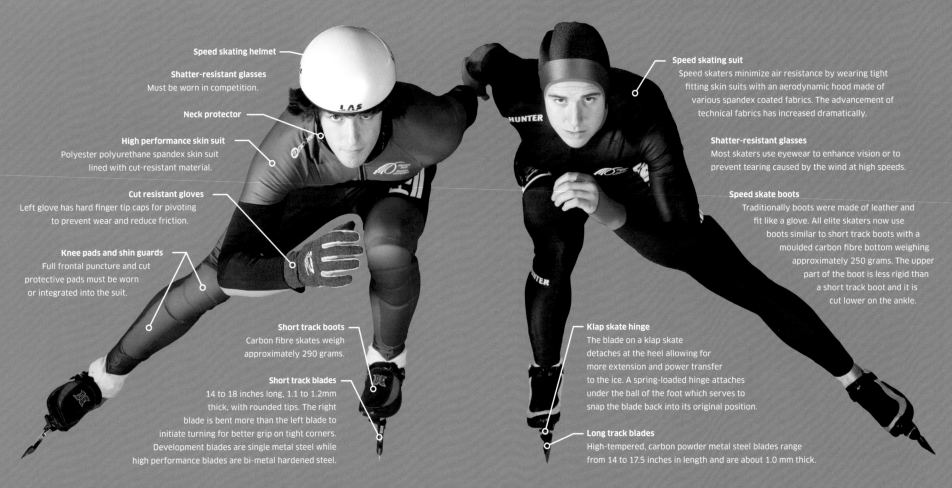

Speed skating helmet

Shatter-resistant glasses
Must be worn in competition.

Neck protector

High performance skin suit
Polyester polyurethane spandex skin suit lined with cut-resistant material.

Cut resistant gloves
Left glove has hard finger tip caps for pivoting to prevent wear and reduce friction.

Knee pads and shin guards
Full frontal puncture and cut protective pads must be worn or integrated into the suit.

Short track boots
Carbon fibre skates weigh approximately 290 grams.

Short track blades
14 to 18 inches long, 1.1 to 1.2mm thick, with rounded tips. The right blade is bent more than the left blade to initiate turning for better grip on tight corners. Development blades are single metal steel while high performance blades are bi-metal hardened steel.

Speed skating suit
Speed skaters minimize air resistance by wearing tight fitting skin suits with an aerodynamic hood made of various spandex coated fabrics. The advancement of technical fabrics has increased dramatically.

Shatter-resistant glasses
Most skaters use eyewear to enhance vision or to prevent tearing caused by the wind at high speeds.

Speed skate boots
Traditionally boots were made of leather and fit like a glove. All elite skaters now use boots similar to short track boots with a moulded carbon fibre bottom weighing approximately 250 grams. The upper part of the boot is less rigid than a short track boot and it is cut lower on the ankle.

Klap skate hinge
The blade on a klap skate detaches at the heel allowing for more extension and power transfer to the ice. A spring-loaded hinge attaches under the ball of the foot which serves to snap the blade back into its original position.

Long track blades
High-tempered, carbon powder metal steel blades range from 14 to 17.5 inches in length and are about 1.0 mm thick.

Lead-in to Lillehammer

1994 World Sprint Championships January 28-30, 1994

94

Two weeks before the 1994 Winter Olympic Games in Lillehammer, Norway, the Olympic Oval and the Organizing Committee hosted the World Sprint Championships. Home-away-from-home Americans Dan Jansen and Bonnie Blair won the sprint titles in the men's and women's categories respectively. Jansen topped off this win by also breaking the world record in the 500-metre with a time of 35.76 seconds and Blair swept all four women's events. Both set world records for sammelagt total points.

Blair and Jansen were close friends and the double victory was a special moment for both of them. At the Calgary Games, Jansen fell in both the 500 and 1000-metre races shortly after hearing his sister had succumbed to leukemia. This time, things were different. Dan and Bonnie skated an emotional victory lap together in the building that had contributed so much to their careers and where they had experienced so many memorable moments.

Fun Fact

Post competition celebrations were often held at Symons Valley Ranch showcasing Calgary's pride in our western heritage and hospitality. Athletes and referees were introduced to line dancing, two-stepping and mechanical bronc riding.

"My only regret is that the Olympic Oval wasn't around when I was a little younger."

– Susan Auch

Developing Champions

XVII Olympic Winter Games Lillehammer, Norway – February 12-27, 1994

The Olympic Games in Lillehammer were the first glimmer of what was to come for the long track team, whose success was founded on the strength of the programs at the Olympic Oval.

94 Lillehammer was the first Games since the Oval's doors opened where an Olympic Oval skater medalled in a long track event. This win came with Susan Auch's silver medal performance in the 500-metre sprint. Auch, who began her career as a short track speed skater, also won a bronze medal in the 3000-metre relay demonstration short track event in Calgary in 1988.

Lillehammer was also the first Winter Olympics where the short track skaters from the newly established Olympic Oval western national short track training centre competed. Derrick Campbell made his first appearance in Olympic competition in Lillehammer, with solid finishes in the 500-metre and 1000-metre individual events (11th and 6th place respectively), and an impressive 4th place as a member of the men's relay team.

And finally, the 1994 Olympics saw a serendipitous and poignant finish to a story that began at the Oval during the 1988 Calgary Games. In a story-book ending to his Olympic career, Dan Jansen – who had never won an Olympic medal despite being one of the best speed skaters in the world for a decade, clocked a world-record time and took home a gold medal in the 1000-metre competition.

Canadian and Olympic Oval skater Kevin Scott was a contender for a medal going into this 1000-metre race as he had set the world record in 1993, shortly before the Games. This was the first world record set by a Canadian at the Olympic Oval. Kevin did not medal in Lillehammer, but took home a gold medal at the World Championships later that season.

Oval Trained Athletes in Lillehammer

- **Speed Skating:** Susan Auch, Mike Hall, Mike Ireland, Sean Ireland, Linda Johnson Blair, Patrick Kelly, Catriona Le May Doan, Ingrid Liepa, Neal Marshall, Michelle Morton, John Kevin Scott

- **Short Track:** Derrick Campbell, Stephen Gough

Along with these Canadian Olympians many athletes, coaches and support staff called the Oval home prior to participating in these Olympics.

Susan Auch

Olympic Oval Wall of Champions Inductee 2003

Susan was born in Winnipeg, Manitoba and was a member of both the short and long track Canadian national speed skating teams over the course of her career. Susan's speed skating career began at the age of nine skating on her family's back yard rink with her brother Derrick. She went on to train at the Olympic Oval and was later coached by Derrick as well. Auch has influenced a legion of young speed skaters from her home town, including fellow Oval athletes Cindy Klassen, Clara Hughes, Shannon Rempel, and Brittany Schussler.

During the 1988 Olympic Games she won a bronze medal as a member of the short track relay team during the demonstration 3000-metre women's relay event. She switched to long track after the 1988 Olympics. Her transition was partly inspired by seeing the newly built Olympic Oval at the Games and wanting to train on the 400-metre track indoors. She moved to Calgary from Manitoba to train and the Oval helped push her to excel in her newly chosen speed skating discipline.

Being part of the Olympic Oval family continuously motivated Susan as she saw other athletes committed to high standards and striving to "Be Better". The ice-makers, operations staff and support programs in sports medicine, physiology, and sports science also inspired her to succeed. She saw a creative team working together to support her efforts and the efforts of other high performance athletes, and this dedication impelled her to train harder. She learned not to set limits and to dream of possibilities.

She represented Canada at four Olympic Games as a member of the Canadian long track team, including Albertville (1992), Lillehammer (1994), Nagano (1998) and Salt Lake City (2002). She won two Olympic silver medals and numerous world cup and World Championship medals as well.

She was named Athlete of the Year six times by the Canadian Amateur Speed Skating Association and inducted into the Manitoba Sports Hall of Fame in 2003. She was inducted on to the Olympic Oval Wall of Champions at the Essent ISU World Cup in the same year.

Susan continues to support the sport of speed skating, volunteering her time as a director on the board of Speed Skating Canada and supporting the Winnipeg speed skating clubs, where her career began.

Career Highlights

- 3 Olympic medals (includes 1988 short track demonstration event bronze)
- 6-time Canadian Amateur Speed Skating Association Athlete of the Year
- Bobby Rosenfeld Canadian Female Athlete of the Year
- Long track oval in Winnipeg named the Susan Auch Oval
- Manitoba Order of the Buffalo Hunt (Order of Manitoba)
- Manitoba Sports Hall of Fame Inductee
- Olympic Oval Wall of Champions Inductee

Celebrity Races

Over the years, the Olympic Oval has held a number of exciting races between celebrities and high performance athletes, as well as media challenges and fun speed skating events.

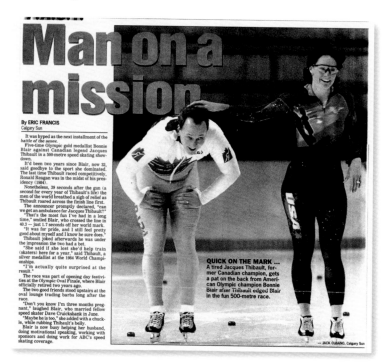

Man on a mission

By ERIC FRANCIS
Calgary Sun

It was hyped as the next installment of the *battle of the sexes.*

Five-time Olympic gold medallist Bonnie Blair against Canadian legend Jacques Thibault in a 500-metre speed skating showdown.

It'd been two years since Blair, now 32, said goodbye to the sport she dominated. The last time Thibault raced competitively, Ronald Reagan was in the midst of his presidency (1984).

Nonetheless, 39 seconds after the gun (a second for every year of Thibault's life) the men of the world breathed a sigh of relief as Thibault roared across the finish line first.

The announcer promptly declared, "can we get an ambulance for Jacques Thibault?"

"That's the most fun I've had in a long time," smiled Blair, who crossed the line in 40.3 — just 1.7 seconds off her world mark.

"It was for pride, and I still feel pretty good about myself and I know he sure does."

Thibault joked afterwards he was under the impression the two had a bet.

"She said if she lost she'd help train (skaters) here for a year," said Thibault, a silver medallist at the 1984 World Championships.

"I'm actually quite surprised at the result."

The race was part of opening day festivities at the Olympic Oval Finale, where Blair officially retired two years ago.

The two good friends stood upstairs at the oval lounge trading barbs long after the race.

"Don't you know I'm three months pregnant," laughed Blair, who married fellow speed skater Dave Cruickshank in June.

"Maybe he is too," she added with a chuckle, while rubbing Thibault's belly.

Blair is now busy helping her husband, doing motivational speaking, working with sponsors and doing work for ABC's speed skating coverage.

QUICK ON THE MARK ...
A tired Jacques Thibault, former Canadian champion, gets a pat on the back from American Olympic champion Bonnie Blair after Thibault edged Blair in the fun 500-metre race.

— JACK CUSANO, Calgary Sun

Our Roomies

The Olympic Oval fosters a holistic approach to sport by partnering with like minded organizations.

Canadian Sport Centre Calgary (CSCC)

 The Canadian Sport Centre Calgary has been at the U of C since its inception April 4, 1994. The mandate of the Sport Centre is to provide a world-class training environment to elite athletes and coaches from across the country. It is part of a network of seven regional Canadian Centres.

From the beginning, the organization was provided space in the Olympic Oval. The first office was for administration and then another was added to house the Athlete Resource Centre "Room with a View." This provided a common area for athletes and coaches to build relationships with other athletes and to access Life Services, a series of programs and workshops that ensure athletes are prepared for their lives beyond sport.

Including the speed skaters that call the Olympic Oval home, over 300 athletes from many different sports under the umbrella of the Canadian Sport Centre train at the Oval using the running track, ice surfaces and weight room facilities. Because of this, a strong bond has formed between the two partners. Resources are shared and each draws on the other's energy and knowledge. The Sport Centre brings a comprehensive and integrated approach to training in the facility – with athletes and coaches working closely with internationally renowned sport experts to create world-class performances and results.

In the early 1990s, Canada was struggling on the world stage with many athletes falling just below medal performances. The Canadian Sport Centre Calgary established a mission to take these athletes from participation to podium finishes by providing leading expertise in the fields of sport science, sport medicine, strength and conditioning, biomechanics, nutrition, mental performance, coach education and life services.

National Coaching Institute (NCI)

 The CSCC also provides coach education and mentoring through the National Coaching Institute (NCI). The NCI fosters and develops excellence in coaching by providing the knowledge and skills for high performance coaches, resulting in Level Four Coaching Certification. The program is competency-based, integrating classroom study with a coaching practicum under the leadership of a sport specific Master Coach. Additionally the CSCC coordinates and delivers various coach education modules for local coaches through the National Coaching Certification Program (NCCP).

The NCI has been pivotal in the development and training of many of the coaches, past and present, in the Oval Program and the Oval family.

Fun Fact

Oval coaches in cycling, women's hockey, and speed skating constitute one of the largest groups of NCI coaching students.

Dale Henwood

Dale has been at the helm of the Canadian Sport Centre Calgary from the beginning. His vision of creating a world-class team of experts to support athletes and coaches training in Alberta has enabled the advancement of sport province-wide and on a national scale. His partnership approach to building the first centre in the network is a huge part of what has made it so successful.

Speed Skating Canada (SSC)

Speed Skating Canada is the governing body for Canadian speed skating, administering the national long track and short track speed skating teams (including the national development teams). The national long track teams have trained at the Oval since 1987 and select short track athletes made the facility home starting with the establishment of the national short track training centre in the 1990s.

Speed Skating Canada staff and coaches share office space with the Olympic Oval staff and coaches, and the national teams participate in daily training sessions on the Oval ice. There is a natural synergy between SSC and the Olympic Oval as the two organizations are focused on athlete development, research and the success of Canadian speed skaters competing on the national and international stage.

Fun Fact

Speed Skating Canada's 125th anniversary overlapped with the Olympic Oval's 25th anniversary celebrations in the 2012-2013 season. The Oval's third floor is home to the SSC Hall of Fame.

The national team athletes benefit greatly from having an indoor venue in which to train, and Oval Program athletes benefit from being exposed to the national team program. The Oval Program is the precursor to the national team programs. Many of the Oval Program coaches have worked for SSC coaching national team athletes to podium finishes.

This symbiotic relationship has resulted in a legacy of excellence in Canadian speed skating, producing world champions and Olympic medallists over the past 25 years. The relationship will continue for years to come as Canadian speed skaters continue to train and compete at the Olympic Oval to be the best in the world.

Alberta Amateur Speed Skating Association (AASSA)

The Alberta Amateur Speed Skating Association is the umbrella organization for the sport of speed skating in Alberta and provides support and resources to ensure the optimal development of provincial athletes at all levels of the sport. The relationship between the Oval and AASSA was established early on, and the two organizations have partnered over the last 25 years to train athletes and host competitions in the facility.

AASSA is the provincial member of Speed Skating Canada, and collaborates with local club coaches, Olympic Oval coaches and Speed Skating Canada's high performance and development staff to structure a development pathway for athletes to achieve the highest level of performance possible. Through AASSA, Alberta's up-and-coming speed skaters access high performance training at the Olympic Oval.

In addition, AASSA runs short track and long track competitions at the facility each season, including the Alberta Open long track event and the RU Fast short track competition. RU Fast is historically one of the largest competitions of the year.

Calgary Speed Skating Association (CSSA)

The Calgary Speed Skating Association (CSSA) was established in 1975 and now trains over 200 skating members of all ages, from recreational skaters to high performance athletes. The Olympic Oval established a partnership with the Calgary club even before the covered oval was built, and the facility was established as a practice venue for club skaters after the 1988 Games.

CSSA is unique from any other club in Canada as their athletes are privileged to train at the Olympic Oval alongside Oval Program and national team athletes. Calgary club skaters train at the best facility in the country, under optimal indoor conditions, on The Fastest Ice in the World™. Coaches for CSSA programs are certified under the National Coaching Certification Program (NCCP) and many are former and current provincial and national team members.

Regularly competing at local, inter-club meets as well as at the highest levels in provincial, national and international competitions, club skaters who train at the Oval act as feeders to provincial, Oval and national team programs.

Community Events

Long Running Annual Events

Family Day

The first Olympic Oval Family Day Skate was held the same year Premier Don Getty declared the Family Day public holiday for Alberta. The Family Day Skate is still an annual tradition at the Oval, with the 2011-2013 events sponsored by Intact Insurance. Prior to 2011, the event was sponsored by Papa John's Pizza.

Halloween

For many years the Oval hosted a Halloween Howl, featuring costumed party goers and decorations. The tunnel was sometimes transformed into a haunted cavern, and even Ollie dressed up!

Olympic Oval Family Christmas Skate

Olympic Oval Family Christmas Skate is an annual tradition. Canada Safeway was the first sponsor. The event features skating with Santa, and invites families to share in the joy of the season on The Fastest Ice in the World™.

Stride and Glide

Stride and Glide started in 1991 and lasted three seasons. Approximately 70 participants took part in the combined 10km run and 10km skate. The purpose of the event was to involve the community in a fun fitness event at the Oval.

Rick Hansen Man in Motion

The Rick Hansen Man in Motion Relay made its first stop at the Olympic Oval in June of 2003. On February 27, 2012 the Relay celebrated its own 25th anniversary right alongside the 25th anniversary of the Olympic Oval, stopping at the facility to spread its message of hope, to create an accessible, inclusive world and find a cure for spinal cord injury, to a crowd of supporters.

Cassie Campbell Street Hockey Festival

The Cassie Campbell Street Hockey Festival (CCSHF) is an annual event held to benefit Ronald McDonald House of Southern Alberta, which provides temporary, affordable accommodation for families whose children are being treated at Calgary medical facilities. Cassie (an Oval Female Hockey Program alumni) founded the event, which has raised $3-million for the House since its inception 10 years ago.

Olympic Oval Senior's Skate

Senior's Skate made its debut in 1994. The third Thursday of every month the seniors of Calgary, Red Deer, Lethbridge and Edmonton would descend on the Oval for this special public skate. The event attracted between 200 and 500 participants per month. They would often bring homemade treats for the staff and were very particular about setting the mood with specific music.

The Toughest Calgarian Alive

The Toughest Calgarian Alive (TCA) competition began as part of the World Police and Fire Games. The University of Calgary adopted the model of the event and renamed it to give it a local angle. The first TCA competition was held at the Olympic Oval in 1994 and continued until 1999. The event consisted of eight events back-to-back, starting with a 5km cross-country run. A shot put event followed, along with a 100-metre dash, 100-metre swim, arms-only rope climb, bench press, consecutive chin-ups and an obstacle course. It was scored much like a decathlon, where a specific performance was worth a certain amount of points. The most points overall won. The competition was also held as part of the World Police and Fire Games in 1997, also held at the Olympic Oval.

Hullaballoo

Hullabaloo was a large indoor carnival and was the brain child of Lou Zaganelli, an employee at William Roper Hull Home. It was initially held at the grounds of Hull Home. After being rained out a few times it moved to the Oval in 1992. Power, Power, Power! For Oval staff, this was the biggest challenge of the event. Everyone wanted power. Breakers tripped, a spider-web of extension cords ran across the floor. The event drew HUGE crowds, close to 7,000 people on average. The last Hullabaloo was held in May of 2000.

Between Friends
Skate-a-Kid-to-Camp

The event started in 1994, and raised money to subsidize registration fees for Camp Bonaventure, which allows children between the ages of 6 and 20 with mental and physical disabilities to experience the outdoors and to build new friendships. Teams of between four and eight members would take turns carrying a baton around the 400-metre Oval ice in a relay-style race.

Alberta Volleyball

Alberta Volleyball has hosted the Canadian West Open at the Oval since May 1998, with one year off in 2012 when the event was hosted in Toronto. The tournament started with 115 teams and grew to 280 teams by 2011. The event draws over 5,000 spectators on average, with 4,000 athletes and coaches. The largest set up for Alberta Volleyball was 22 volleyball courts inside the Olympic Oval.

Driven Car Show

What started as the Driven to Performance Car Show was rebranded in 2012 as simply Driven. An indoor trade and car show representing western Canada's best rides, local and national exhibitors, and a huge stage show, the event has packed the Oval with over 275 show vehicles each spring since 2007.

Calgary Cares AIDS Benefit

The Calgary Cares Benefit was held at the Oval for the first time in 2007. Michelle Ladouceur, event chair, and Dan Holinda, executive director AIDS Calgary, created this night of hope to benefit AIDS Calgary programs and initiatives. The 2007 event at the Olympic Oval raised $40,000 through ticket sales and a silent auction, whose highlight was the celebrity blue jean jacket auction – featuring jackets signed by Mick Jagger, Eddie Murphy, Bon Jovi, Diana Ross, Elton John and Gloria Estefan.

Monday Night Skate

Nearly every Monday night of the public skating season since 1992, community members have been invited to skate for free at the Oval with a donation of a non-perishable food item. Between 2000 and 2012, 134,823 pounds of food has been collected. The initiative began as a way for the Olympic Oval to give back to the community and welcome public skating participants to the facility free of charge with a donation to the Food Bank.

Calgary Co-op saw the value of this community investment and joined the Olympic Oval as presenting partner of the Monday Night Skate in 2008. In 2010, the weekly skate was rebranded as "Calgary Co-op Skate-to-Win" and this continues to today.

The tradition of bringing a non-perishable food item for a free skate remains, and participants can still enjoy a free session of skating on the Fastest Ice in the World™ with a donation of a featured Calgary Co-op product of the month. Attendees are also entered to win monthly prizes and a grand prize of a $1,000 shopping spree at Calgary Co-op.

The Monday night skate is the Oval's most popular public skating event of the season.

Year-by-Year Breakdown in Pounds

• 2000	11,013	• 2007	11,610
• 2001	7,613	• 2008	10,010
• 2002	8,342	• 2009	17,150
• 2003	9,060	• 2010	14,770
• 2004	7,402	• 2011	10,306
• 2005	10,673	• 2012	7,150
• 2006	9,724		

Public Skating and
Public Running

In addition to community events throughout the year, the Olympic Oval has been holding regular public skating and public running sessions in the facility since the early years. These public hours give the community at large an opportunity to experience how special the Oval is and what it has to offer.

Paul Harris Rotary Luncheon, June 22, 1996 — More than 4,000 Rotarians sat down to lunch at the Olympic Oval for the Paul Harris Rotary Luncheon. Each person attending the event had contributed at least $1,000 to the Rotary Foundation, whose programs finance initiatives to improve the quality of life worldwide. A six-piece band called the Dixieland Knights and Dan-the-One-Man-Band roamed through the crowd while they played. Jokers, buskers and jugglers on stilts also wandered among the tables. The event was the largest annual Harris luncheon and stands as a record for the most people ever to eat a sit-down meal at the Olympic Oval.

Selected Community Events

1989 • Exhibition Calgary Kickers Soccer Game – In 1989, the Oval was a multi-use venue. The space was booked for a major league exhibition soccer game in the summer of 1989. The Calgary Kickers competed against a professional team from Sheffield, England at this event. The U of C Varsity football team was recruited to install the artificial turf, as they were the only ones capable of pulling the heavy carpet across the floor. Still, the installation took six weeks.

1990 • Ringette Nationals, Apr. 9-14, 1990 – The 10-team tournament was nationally televised on CTV's Wide World of Sports.
• Gymnastics Nationals

1991 • Broomball Competition, Master Athlete Winter Games, Feb. 15-16, 1991

1992 • Silver Auctions Collector Car Auction, Apr. 25, 1992
• 18th annual Canadian National Netball Championships, May 14-18, 1992

1993 • Royal Canadian Navy Reunion

1994 • Skate-a-Kid-to-Camp
• Silver Car Auction
• Hullabaloo
• National Sports Center Kick-Off

1995 • Stride and Glide

1996 • Calgary Model Boat Racing Association
• Olympic Hall of Fame Ice Gala

1997 • World Police and Fire Games

1998 • Olympic Oval hosts Olympic bid committee for 2002 Winter Olympic Games, Sept. 1998

1999 • Y2K year 2000 event – Jim Hunter built a toboggan hill on the north ice for New Year's Eve, Dec. 31, 1999
• Rhythmic Gymnastics Competition
• Cars 4 Kid's Cancer Show and Shine, May 29-30, 1999

2003 • Canada Wide Science Fair, May 17, 2003 – Students from grades 7 to 12 from across Canada showed off their scientific projects, ranging in topics from medical research to environmental studies, to engineering and computer technology.
• Robot Challenge

2005 • Calgary's Child Magazine Family Fun Fair, Apr. 30, 2005
• Solar Challenge

| 2006 | • Alberta Volleyball Association | 2009 | • Canada West Open Volleyball Tournament |

2007 • A Ship in Full Sail (Shell Canada)

• SML Pool Tournament

2008 • Juno FanFare Meet-and-Greet, Apr. 5, 2008 – Thousands packed the Olympic Oval for an extended autograph session and the chance to meet their favourite Canadian music acts. Juno nominees Hedley, Theory of a Deadman, Jully Black, Joel Plaskett and Jill Barber were some of the artists in attendance.
• Canadian Gymnastics Championships

2010 • Cassie Campbell Street Hockey Festival

2012 • Chinook City Roller Derby Flat Track Fever. Held in 2012 and 2013.
• Calgary Youth Science Fair. Held in 2012 and 2013.
• Driven Car Show

2013 • First Robotics Competition (FRC), Apr. 5-6, 2013
• NAGVA Tournament, May 24-26, 2013

Olympic Oval H1N1 Clinic Serves High-Risk Calgarians

On October 28, 2009, the University of Calgary opened the fifth public H1N1 vaccination clinic in Calgary on the third floor observation deck of the Olympic Oval. The additional clinic was opened after a request from Alberta Health Services, as the four existing H1N1 vaccination clinics were approaching wait times of four and five hours. The Olympic Oval clinic had a primary mandate to serve high-risk Calgarians.

Faculty, staff and students were also encouraged to get vaccinated, but were asked to wait 24 to 48 hours after the clinic's opening to give high risk individuals (pregnant women, children between 6 months and 10 years of age, seniors, and immuno-compromised) priority. The clinic stayed open from October 28 to November 20, 2009.

Women's Hockey

Olympic Oval International High Performance Female Hockey Program Begins

Women's hockey came to the Oval in 1995 with Cathy Priestner Allinger's vision to implement a high performance female hockey program that would develop elite athletes and grow the women's game. Adding hockey players to the mix of athletes who were already training at the Oval was in line with the philosophy of fostering a multi-disciplinary environment at the facility. Female hockey in Canada at the time was underfunded and struggled to find resources.

Shannon Miller, the coach of the women's national team, and her colleague Kathy Berg, were in Calgary operating a female hockey school and coaching a senior AAA women's hockey team. They wanted to move their hockey school to the University of Calgary campus. The timing was perfect. They pitched their concept to Priester Allinger and the U of C, who both accepted the idea.

A five-year plan was hatched to design an International High Performance Female Hockey Program (IHPFHP) to attract the best athletes to the facility. The three women worked tirelessly to make the innovative, first-of-its-kind program fly.

Adding to the perfect storm of events was the upcoming 1998 Olympic Winter Games in Nagano, Japan, where women's hockey would be included for the first time. Leading up to the official start of a centralized pre-Olympic season, Shannon Miller worked as a volunteer with Hockey Canada.

Even though women's hockey was a fast-growing sport in the mid-90s, it was inadequately funded and a paid employee was not an option. The commitment, time and energy Miller gave to growing the sport cannot be understated. Cathy Priestner Allinger fought hard for funding and secured money for a paid, permanent staff member. Miller

was offered the position and took a leave from her day job as a police officer to coach hockey full-time.

The Oval program accepted highly skilled women who were part-time players and gave them the opportunity to live and play like full-time NHL players, without the pay. The IHPFHP was built into three training levels (midget, junior and senior) and two teams (the Oval Lightning development team and Oval X-Treme elite team). The U of C Dinos women's team also evolved out of the program. They trained 11 months of the year.

In addition to training Canadian players, the program worked with some of the best international athletes from the United States, Japan, Germany, Finland, Switzerland, China and Australia. It kept many elite players in the game by pushing them to compete at an even higher level. Like the speed skating programs, the women's hockey program built a family of athletes who would be connected to the Oval for years to come.

First Hockey Camp

The first female midget hockey camp was held at the Oval in the summer of 1995. It attracted mostly local female minor hockey players who wanted to enhance their on-ice skills and mental game.

The Evolution of the Oval Female Hockey Program

The women's hockey program started with seven full time athletes in 1995 and grew to include 60 players by 1997. By early 2000 there were nearly 200 athletes in the three training groups and three teams. High performance players were competing at midget, senior and elite levels. The U of C Dinos Varsity team also formed and joined the family of female hockey players practicing on the south rink. With the Nagano Olympics only a year away, Shannon Miller left her position as director of the Oval hockey program to focus solely on coaching the Olympic team. Kathy Berg stepped in to take her place as director.

Through the next decade the program continued to explode, attracting the best players and the best people, committed to the development of the women's game. They were passionate and focused on a common goal – to be the best in the world. The Olympic Oval supported their mission providing opportunities for them to learn and grow through the multi-faceted approach cultivated at the facility from the beginning.

Over the 14-year history of the Olympic Oval International High Performance Female Hockey Program its players were part of every championship and medal-winning team in Canadian women's hockey. These Canadian teams dominated, and continue to dominate the sport to this day. The Oval women's program lives on through these players, past and present, who were part of building the legacy of women's hockey in this country.

Staff and Coaches over the Years

- Mario Amantea
- Andrew Barron
- Michelle Belanger
- Kathy Berg
- Tim Bothwell
- Lisa Brown
- Steve Carlyle
- Chris Chisamore
- Danielle Choquet
- Bart Doan
- Julie Healy
- Sandy Johnson
- Bjorn Kindling
- Wally Kozak
- Leah Lacroix
- Marcel Lacroix
- Tracey Luhowy
- Steve Martell
- Robin McDonald
- Steve McCarthy
- Shannon Miller
- Tomas Pacina
- Jason Poole
- Alison Ramsley
- Danièle Sauvageau
- Catherine Vandoorslaer
- Clare Wilson

Female Hockey Program Highlights

1997
- Inaugural year for Dinos Women's Hockey Team.
- In April of 1997, many of the Oval players played in or attended the exciting World Championships in Kitchener, Ontario. The Canadians won in overtime with a 4-3 score over the Americans before more than 6,000 spectators.

1998
- U of C hosts the first ever CIAU Western Conference Women's Hockey Championships.
- Tournament MVPs included Oval hockey program athletes: forward Kelly Bechard, defence Colleen Sostorics and Cindy Klassen. Klassen, who at the time played hockey for the Manitoba team, would soon commit her athleticism to speed skating and move to Calgary to train at the Oval, ultimately becoming the most decorated Canadian Olympic athlete in history.
- Oval hosts first female midget hockey tournament.

1999
- Addition of Junior Women's Hockey Program.
- Acceptance of female hockey into the National Sports School.

2005
- The Oval leads the drive to create the Western Women's Hockey League (WWHL) and hosts the first WWHL Championship.
- Oval X-Treme play Calgary Flames Alumni for the first time and raise $10,000 for charity Goal on Sight. Battle of the Border series sees Oval X-Treme defeat the US Selects, raising $101,000 for minor hockey and local charities.

2006
- Canadian women's hockey team wins gold medal at 2006 Winter Olympics. Six Oval female hockey players are on this winning team.

2007
- Former National Team member, Calgary Oval X-Treme player and Olympic flag bearer Danielle Goyette starts her rookie season coaching, leading the Dinos women's team to the Alberta Colleges Athletic Conference (ACAC) finals.

2012
- Jumping forward to March 2012, Goyette coaches the Dinos to their first-ever Canada West and Canadian Interuniversity Sport (CIS) titles. Led by Team Canada captain Hayley Wickenheiser, the U of C Dinos rode an 18-game winning streak to their first-ever national title defeating Montreal in the gold medal game. The Dinos won the championship after just three seasons in CIS competition following a seven-year stint in the ACAC.

World Dominance

The torch is passed – Jacques Thibault named General Manager

97

In 1997 Jacques Thibault was named general manager of the Olympic Oval. Jacques started working at the facility in May of 1988, shortly after the Olympic Games. He came to the Oval to coach the national long track speed skating team and remained in this position until 1990. At that point, he accepted the position of program manager under the leadership of Cathy Priestner Allinger. Jacques developed the Oval Programs in long track and short track speed skating. He was also pivotal in the additions of high performance female hockey and the national cycling centre.

As general manager Jacques continued to build on the team approach he embraced in his previous roles. His philosophy on sports development was one that supported the idea of a multi-disciplinary approach and partner collaboration. He firmly believed that athletes would benefit from a variety of sports training in one place, feeding off each other's energy. This synergistic path involved bringing the provincial speed skating clubs, the national speed skating organization, CODA and others to the table to build a facility that was without duplication of services and efficiently served elite athletes.

He also drew new users into the facility by building interest from the ground up. From the beginning, Thibault focused on reaching out to schools to recruit skaters to the speed skating club and Olympic Oval programs. He partnered with U of C Campus Recreation to invite their clients to come experience speed skating. He wanted to see people using the facility to create energy and buzz.

During his tenure, Jacques Thibault was a tireless advocate and architect of ideas. He took every opportunity to attend international events and spread the word about what was going on at the facility. He was instrumental in the creation of Olympic Oval Finale and Saturday races, which continue to this day. He championed research and development of new technologies as he knew that excellence could not be achieved in mediocre conditions.

Much of Thibault's work was geared to one goal – winning. He wanted success for the facility and its athletes worldwide. The realization of this goal came to a climax during the 1998 Winter Olympics in Nagano. These Olympic Games were the beginning of great success for Canadian speed skaters. The Olympic Oval shined with unprecedented medal performances and world records. Added to that, the Oval was the place to be, with athletes, media and fans turning up at the building day and night – even in their pyjamas – to watch Oval-trained athletes compete in the Winter Olympic Games live from Nagano, Japan.

In 2004, a year before he left his position as general manager, Thibault participated in the development of the Own the Podium 2010 program and co-wrote the Fast Track to Turin 2006 program that lead to the most successful Winter Olympics in Canada's history at the time.

The Oval was instrumental in providing the world an understanding that Canadian athletes are capable of podium performances across all sports, both summer and winter.

Oval Shines

1997 Sets the Tone – World Records Fall at World Single Distance Championships

Klap skates changed the world of long track speed skating forever. At the pre-Olympic World Single Distance Championships held at the Olympic Oval in November of 1997 it was anticipated that skating under the best ice conditions in the world, and the new toe-hinged design skate would help skaters achieve the fastest times in history and world records were expected to fall. The prediction was right.

On November 25, 1997 the speed skating world watched as athletes shattered world records at the two-day competition on the Oval ice. On the first day, Bonnie Blair watched from the stands as Catriona Le May Doan broke Blair's world record of 38.69 with a time of 37.90 seconds in the 500-metre sprint. Le May Doan also set a world record in the 1000-metre race that same day, skating 1.16.07. This record was beaten the next day as American Chris Witty skated a time of 1.15.43.

There were 120 skaters from 25 countries at the event. A total of eight world records were broken in two days.

Dutch "Make-a-Wish" Teen

During the 1997 championships, 16-year old Johannes van der Velde was granted his wish of skating with his speed skating heroes, Dutch Olympic medallist and World All-Round Champion Gianni Romme and Canadian national team skater Sylvain Bouchard on The Fastest Ice in the World™. Van der Velde was stricken with a degenerative muscle disease, and his trip to Calgary was arranged by a Dutch organization similar to Canada's Make-a-Wish Foundation.

Cycling Rolls In

The National Cycling Training & Development Centre (NCC) was founded in 1997.

 The goal of the centre was to provide a year-round training environment for cyclists in all of the Olympic cycling disciplines: mountain biking, track racing and road racing (in 2005, BMX was added to the program with Tanya Dubnicoff as the first national team BMX head coach). It established four program levels, including high performance, advanced, club racing and new riders (for juniors under 19 years). Under the leadership of Jacques Thibault, the program became an official Oval program in 1997.

Former speed skater and cyclist Kurt Innes was hired as the first head coach for the centre. As the leader of the cycling program from 1997 to 2003, Innes had the opportunity to work with athletes such as Tanya Dubnicoff, Jim Fisher, Doug Baron and Jennie Reed and lead them to international podium performances.

The program was truly ground-breaking in the cycling world in Canada. Prior to the Oval program being established, Canadian cyclists went south to train outdoors in warmer climates. The NCC gave them a dedicated training environment in their own country. The Oval purchased electronic start gates for athletes to perfect their starts and they were provided access to the high performance weight room, running track, and the best strength and technical coaches. Finally, like the Oval speed skating programs, the cycling program accepted international athletes where other Canadian programs would not.

The NCC Calgary produced outstanding results right out of the gate and the momentum continued into the mid-2000s. Starting in the late 1990s with Olympian, multiple World Championships medallist, PanAm and Commonwealth Games gold medallist Tanya Dubnicoff, through to PanAm Championships gold medallists Jim Fisher and Doug Baron in the later years, the cycling program at the Oval was a true testament to the success of the facility's multi-sport environment. The NCC Calgary supported international podium performances between 1997 and 2003, and played a critical role in fostering the growth of junior and development level athletes for future international podium success. Athletes such as: 2006 Commonwealth Games medallist Travis Smith; World Championships medallist Laura Brown; 2012 Olympian Monique Sullivan; and two-time Olympian, multiple World Championships medallist Zach Bell all honed their cycling talents as members of the NCC Calgary program.

The cycling program also provided mentorship opportunities and a professional environment for cycling coaches to learn and develop into world-class coaches. Tanya Dubnicoff (national cycling team, 2008 and 2012 Olympic coach), Dan Proulx (national mountain bike coach and Olympic coach London 2012) and Stephen Burke (Paralympic cycling coach Beijing 2008) were all products of the Olympic Oval environment.

Cycling Highlights

1998
- Tanya Dubnicoff wins gold medal at Commonwealth Games (Kuala Lumpur, Malaysia).

1999
- Tanya Dubnicoff wins 2 gold medals at PanAm Games (Winnipeg).
- Doug Baron wins bronze medal at PanAm Games (Winnipeg).

2000
- Tanya Dubnicoff and Jim Fisher represent Canada at 2000 Sydney Summer Olympics.
- Jim Fisher wins gold medal at Pan American Championships.
- NCC Calgary head coach Kurt Innes national cycling team coach at 2000 Summer Olympics.
- Stephen Burke named assistant coach of the Paralympic national cycling team.

2001
- Doug Baron wins gold medal at Pan American Championships.

2002
- Travis Smith makes international debut at Pan American Championships.

2004
- Jeff Sparling, Rene Regimbald, Mark McDonald and Laura Brown debut at the Junior World Championships.

2006
- Monique Sullivan debuts at the Junior World Championships.
- Zach Bell sets new Canadian Pursuit Record at Commonwealth Games.

Pedal to the Medals

The cycling program at the Olympic Oval continued to flourish as the 2008 Summer Olympics in Beijing approached. Zach Bell would represent Canada and the Olympic Oval at these Olympics with a top-10 finish in the men's point race as his best result. Up and coming cyclists also trained at the facility, achieving success on the international stage.

After the Beijing Games, the cycling program was lost due to the upheaval caused by the financial crisis of 2009. Innes left Calgary in January of 2009 and the Oval High Performance Cycling program was dissolved soon after. Like the Oval X-Treme and the Olympic Oval High Performance Women's Hockey program, cycling would not survive the tough times. The loss of the cycling program not only affected the cyclists, but was a sad loss for the other high performance athletes (including the speed skaters) who trained alongside them.

When the new funding agreement for the Oval and the other Olympic legacy venues was secured, the lost programs would not return to the Olympic Oval, but some of the participants would. The Canadian Sport Centre Calgary would continue to run the National Cycling Centre, with the Olympic Oval as home-base. Athletes of all ages and all abilities, from recreational to high performance, would continue to train year-round in road, track, cyclocross, mountain bike and para-cycling. Para-cycling has, over the years, been a stand-out in this program, producing a number of national team and Paralympic medallists since its inception in 1998.

Other athletes excelled internationally as well. At the 2011 PanAm Games, former Olympic Oval Cycling Program athlete Laura Brown won a bronze medal in the individual time trial as an excited Mexican crowd cheered her on. The Oval Jumbotron came alive with congratulations after her win, and her mother Dawn Brown (Olympic Oval staff member) shed tears of joy when she saw the congratulatory message on the Oval screen.

In 2012, at the London Olympics, Oval trained cyclist Monique Sullivan raced in the Women's Sprint (11th place finish) and the Women's Keirin (6th place) under coach Tanya Dubnicoff, Oval alumni and arguably one of the most successful Canadian cyclists in history.

Fun Fact

Jaye Milley and Brayden McDougal, two exceptional Paralympic cyclists train in the Cycling Centre Calgary, Para-cycling program at the Oval. Milley, a quadruple amputee, won a gold and a bronze medal at the 2011 world cup and represented Canada at the 2012 Paralympic Games. McDougal has competed in cycling at two Paralympic Games (Beijing and London) and three World Championships.

Oval Cycling Coaches through the Years

- Phil Abbott
- Stephen Burke
- Tanya Dubnicoff
- Jayson Gillespie
- Kurt Innes
- Dan Proulx

Klap Skate

The klap skate was first introduced in the 1984-1985 speed skating season, but it was not until the late 1990s that the technology was taken seriously.

The first team to really have success with the new skates was the Dutch women's speed skating team, who started using them for the 1996-1997 season. The rest of the world saw this and the following season the skates were commonplace worldwide. The Winter Olympics in Nagano, Japan were the first Olympic Games where klap skates were used.

The traditional speed skate boot features a fixed blade. The klap skate is different as it combines a boot where the blade is hinged at the front, allowing the blade to come away from the heel. The benefit of the design allows longer contact with the ice and requires less energy to go fast. The technology resulted in a torrent of world records being broken at the Olympic Oval.

Many skaters were initially resistant to the new technology. In order to capitalize on the opportunity this new equipment offered, skaters needed to adapt their technique. For some, including those who were "late pushers" (meaning their power came late in the stride), it was highly beneficial and changed their careers.

Fun Fact

Klap skates are named for the 'clapping' noise the blade makes as it comes into contact with the boot.

Research and Technology

Maple Blade

As the klap skate gained momentum in the world of long track, short track coaches and skaters were looking for ways to improve their speed as well. The new hinged mechanism, however, was impractical for short track as it was too dangerous for the tight corners of the small rink. Short track coach Marcel Lacroix took the initiative to research and develop new equipment for his athletes to improve their performances. Marcel shared his solution design ideas with Johan Bennink of the Netherlands, and this led to the start of testing and production of the Maple Blade.

With research and development assistance from the U of C Faculty of Kinesiology High Performance Lab, the Maple Blade was developed. It was unveiled the year of the 1998 Winter Olympics. This equipment upgrade assisted Canada's national short track team in bringing home a gold medal at these Olympics and it subsequently became the standard high performance short track blade worldwide.

A priority at the Olympic Oval is to create an atmosphere that helps athletes be the best they can be. This includes having the best coaches, best ice, best programs, best facility and support.

Some of this support comes from technological advances in the sport of speed skating and beyond. From the very beginning scientists and engineers have been in the building conducting tests and collecting data.

The Quiet Eye

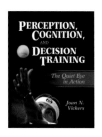

Dr. Joan Vickers was one of the early researchers who used the facility. Before and after the 1988 Winter Olympic Games she (and her team) compiled ice hockey goalie shooting data on the ice at the Oval. This research revealed that prolonged fixations called the "quiet eye" on the stick and puck before release was key to making saves.

Dr. Vickers carried out eye testing and training on athletes in a wide range of sports, for over three decades.

One of her most productive programs was with speed skaters. She used eye trackers and external cameras that synched the gaze of the skaters with their skating strides. This information was then used by coaches to help skaters maintain optimal focus when they raced. Internationally, Canadian speed skaters are known for maintaining their focus under the most demanding of conditions.

For 12 years (1994-2006) Dr. Vickers also introduced the coaches of the Oval to decision training and specific decision making tools that are known to enhance long term athletic performance.

Fun Fact

VH Skates were developed by Oval Program alumni, Scott Van Horne whose first prototype was worn by Mike Ireland in his first world cup medal performance.

"The love of short track speed skating at the Olympic Oval developed into a centre deep in national and international talent, creating a more competitive circuit."

– Derrick Campbell

Gold Rush to Nagano

XVIII Olympic Winter Games, Nagano Japan – February 7-22, 1998

Canada sent 153 athletes to the Games and together they brought home fifteen medals – six of them gold.

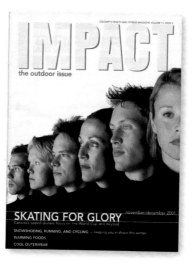

More importantly for the Calgary Olympic Oval, these Games saw exceptional performances from Canadian speed skaters and a medal haul unequalled in the country's speed skating history. The Nagano Olympics were the fruition of Cathy Priestner Allinger's 10-year prediction of excellence from 1988. It was the start of great successes that would continue through to the 2010 Olympics in Vancouver.

Long Track Takes Five

The Canadian long track speed skating team brought home five medals from Nagano. Catriona Le May Doan became the first female Canadian speed skater in history to win a gold medal. She won the women's 500-metre race, with her teammate Susan Auch taking the silver medal in the same event. Catriona also won a bronze medal in the 1000-metre event behind American Chris Witty (silver) and Dutch skater Marianne Timmer (gold).

On the men's side, Jeremy Wotherspoon won silver in the men's 500-metre race, ahead of Kevin Crockett who won the bronze. Hiroyasu Shimizu took the gold medal in the event.

A Golden Moment

Short track speed skaters had equally impressive results. Oval short track program skater Derrick Campbell was a member of the Canadian men's relay team (along with Éric Bédard, Marc Gagnon and François Drolet)

who skated to the first Canadian 5000-metre relay gold medal – one of the most inspiring stories of the Games.

In January, two and a half weeks prior to the Games, Chantal Sevigny and Derrick Campbell crashed during training at the Oval. Campbell ended up with a huge gash in his thigh, requiring 60 stitches and resulting in 10 lost training days. After the crash the Olympics seemed a no-go for Campbell. Three days before the Games the stitches came out and Derrick made the decision to go. He never gave up on his goal of Nagano and came out on the other side with a gold medal.

Oval Hub of the Games

The Olympic Oval was a hub of activity in Calgary during the 1998 Winter Olympics. It

was the place to go for fans, athletes and media to watch races, get the background stories and soak up the spirit and atmosphere of Olympic competition. People even came to the Oval in their pyjamas in the middle of the night to watch live races together.

Athletes Welcomed Home

On Saturday, February 28, 1998 Calgarians welcomed home Canada's speed skating medallists with a party at the Olympic Oval. The crowd was full of young children, inspired to get involved in sports by the success of the speed skaters at the Nagano Games.

SKATING FOR GLORY

Canada's speed skaters focus on the World Cup and beyond

SNOWSHOEING, RUNNING, AND CYCLING — keeping you in shape this winter
WARMING FOODS
COOL OUTERWEAR

Oval Trained Athletes in Nagano

- **Speed Skating:** Susan Auch, Kevin Crockett, Steven Elm, Linda Johnson Blair, Mark Knoll, Catriona Le May Doan, Ingrid Liepa, Kevin Marshall, Neal Marshall, Susan Massitti, Michelle Morton, Cindy Overland, Jeremy Wotherspoon

- **Short Track:** Derrick Campbell, Chantale Sevigny, Tania Vincent

- **Women's Hockey:** Jennifer Botterill, Judy Diduck, Lori Dupuis, Danielle Goyette, Lesley Reddon, Manon Rhéaume, Hayley Wickenheiser, Stacy Wilson

Along with these Canadian Olympians many athletes, coaches and support staff called the Oval home prior to participating in these Olympics.

Catriona Le May Doan

Olympic Oval Wall of Champions Inductee 2003

Catriona arrived at the Olympic Oval from Saskatoon, Saskatchewan to train full time at the age of seventeen. She lived in residence at the U of C, a stone's throw from the facility that would be her home for the next two decades. Self-admittedly, she was intimidated by the change from her life in Saskatchewan, but she would eventually settle into a long career of speed skating triumphs that started on the Oval ice.

Catriona Le May Doan won her first Olympic gold medal in the women's 500-metre event in 1998 at the Nagano Winter Olympics. Later at those Games she added a bronze medal win in the 1000-metre race, which led to her carrying the Canadian flag at the closing ceremonies.

At the following Winter Olympics in 2002 in Salt Lake City, Catriona won another gold in the 500-metre, making her the only Canadian to win back-to-back individual gold medals at the Winter Games.

She finished first overall in the world cup standings in the 500-metre and 1000-metre for the 1998 season. In 1999 she nearly equaled this achievement by finishing first once more in the 500 metres. She dominated the sprints with a victory streak of 20 races over two seasons. In addition, Catriona broke an astonishing 13 world records in her career as a speed skater.

Eleven of her 13 world records were set on The Fastest Ice in the World™ at the Olympic Oval.

Le May Doan attributes her legendary success to her dedication and the commitment of a team of supporters who contributed their knowledge to her training. These individuals are people like U of C sports medicine physician Dr. Dave Smith, who helped her achieve top conditioning through his scientific expertise. He worked with her for 17 years, and led her to podium finishes and world record times. This partnership was a direct reflection of the vision Dr. Roger Jackson had for the Kinesiology Complex and the Oval at the very beginning.

Catriona's numerous coaches were also instrumental in her development as an athlete, inspiring her to strive for excellence, and to push for success in sport and in life.

In addition, like many speed skaters at the Olympic Oval, Le May Doan had the opportunity to train alongside winter and summer athletes in other sports. This cross-pollination fostered communication, bonding, respect, and learning from other disciplines, which ultimately made Catriona a better skater.

After hanging up her skates, Le May Doan continued her involvement in speed skating, and continued to contribute to the Olympic Oval as Associate Director. She is dedicated to the sport, to high performance sport in general, and to continuing the legacy of the Oval as a facility that gives back to the community and welcomes the world through its doors to accept challenges and exceed expectations.

Career Highlights

- 3 Olympic medals
- 3-time Bobbie Rosenfeld Canadian Sport Awards Athlete of the Year
- 13 world records
- Canada's Sports Hall of Fame Inductee
- Canadian Team Flag Bearer Salt Lake Winter Olympic opening ceremony and Nagano Winter Olympic closing ceremonies
- Gemini Award, Best Sports Analyst, Vancouver 2010
- Honourary degrees from University of Calgary, University of Saskatoon, University of Regina
- Lou Marsh Award as Canada's Athlete of the Year
- Officer of the Order of Canada
- Olympic Oval Wall of Champions Inductee
- Torch lighting at Vancouver Winter Games opening and closing ceremonies

She shoots, she scores!

The Olympic Oval women's hockey program was game-changing. The approach to training was different in many ways from the traditional approach to player development.

98 The focus was on a more holistic vision of the sport and developing athletes as individuals. Coaches were encouraged to learn and grow right alongside their players. Emphasis was placed on research, including research on equipment and technology. The players not only trained with the best coaches, but also accessed sport psychology, massage therapy, nutrition support, strength training and were introduced to video feedback and decision training.

Athletes and coaches were encouraged to learn from other sports as well. The hockey players took lessons from the speed skating coaches on improving their stride and power. They learned how to run efficiently from the track and field coaches, with the goal to improve their cardio and speed on the ice.

The Oval Program was also a leader in initiating development internationally, signing a formal agreement with the Chinese National Program to train at the facility within the female high performance program. The top six players from this program remained in Calgary for one year. They trained at the Oval and two players were placed on each of the Oval X-Treme, Edmonton Chimos and Strathmore Rockies teams. This was the first cultivation of international player development in female hockey.

In 2000, the Oval designed and implemented the Australian National Women's Ice Hockey Program. Kathy Berg provided the expertise and coaching and they went on to win a Gold Medal in Div III IIHF World Championships in 2003. This program is still thriving and competing at World Championships.

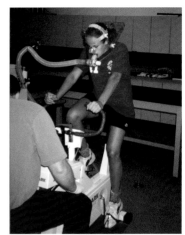

Women's Hockey at the Olympics

The Team Canada squad, some of whose members trained at the Oval under the guidance of Shannon Miller, went into the Nagano Olympics as gold medal favorites, having won four consecutive women's world titles. The United States were their closest rival with four straight world silver medal finishes.

There were six teams competing in Nagano: China, Sweden, Japan, Finland, United States and Canada. Canada and the United States faced off for the gold medal game in a heated competition that ended in a 3-1 victory and a gold medal for the United States.

The Canadian team would eventually go on to win gold at the 2002 Games in Salt Lake City and the 2006 Winter Olympics in Turin.

The women's hockey program at the Olympic Oval ended in 2009 due to funding struggles, but the national team, comprised of many Oval alumni, continued to dominate and won gold again on Canadian soil at the 2010 Vancouver Games.

Featured Athletes

Hayley Wickenheiser

Hayley Wickenheiser started playing hockey at the age of five. She won her first national gold medal as a hockey player for Team Alberta at the Canada Winter Games under-18 Girl's Tournament in 1991. She was 13 years old. She was only 15 when she played for Team Canada in her first international tournament, the 1994 World Championship in Lake Placid.

Hayley is a four-time Olympic medallist, winning silver in Nagano 1998, gold in Salt Lake 2002, gold again in Torino 2006, and a third gold in Vancouver 2010. At the Vancouver Games she read the athlete's oath at the opening ceremonies, an honour that spoke to her outstanding athletic achievements representing Canada on the world stage.

Hayley has the distinction of being the only woman to play with an elite level men's team, HC Salamat in Finland. During their 2003-2004 season, and in her 23 games with the club, she tallied two goals and ten assists.

Wickenheiser is also one of the few athletes to compete in Summer and Winter Olympic Games (along with fellow Oval alumni Clara Hughes). She played softball with

the Canadian women's team at the 2000 Summer Olympics in Sydney.

She has trained at the Olympic Oval for a good part of her career, including as a member of Team Canada, a member of the Oval X-Treme (from 1997-2005), and currently captains the University of Calgary Dinos Varsity team under coach and former teammate, Danielle Goyette. Like many Oval high performance athletes, Wickenheiser also attended U of C as a student, benefitting from the proximity of the high performance training facilities to the educational institution. She graduated in June of 2013 with a Bachelor of Kinesiology with Distinction.

Olympic Oval Wall of Champions, Women's Hockey

- Dana Antal
- Kelly Bechard
- Jennifer Botterill
- Cassie Campbell
- Judy Diduck
- Danielle Goyette
- Lesley Reddon
- Manon Rhéaume
- Colleen Sostorics
- Hayley Wickenheiser
- Stacy Wilson

Danielle Goyette

Danielle Goyette joined the Canadian women's national ice hockey team in 1991. Prior to the 1998 Nagano Olympics, where women's hockey was first included as an Olympic sport, Goyette and the Canadian team won gold medals at the 1992, 1994 and 1997 World Championships. She paved the way in women's hockey, providing inspiration to those who dared to dream big.

Danielle moved to Calgary to train at the Olympic Oval International High Performance Female Hockey Program under coach Shannon Miller. The women's national team squad ultimately centralized to Calgary in 1997 in preparation for the 1998 Nagano Winter Olympic Games. While in Calgary, Goyette trained with the women's national team and was a core member of the Oval X-Treme elite amateur team from 1999 to 2007.

Just prior to the Nagano Games in 1998, Danielle was hit with the terrible news that her father had passed away. With the support of her family, team and coach she decided to compete in the Olympics in memory of her dad. During this difficult time she triumphed and was the nation's top scorer, accumulating eight goals in six games. The Canadian team brought home a silver medal after losing to the United States in the final game.

She was a member of the World Championship gold medal women's team in 1999, 2000, 2001, 2004, and 2007, and the silver medal team in 2005. In 2002, she won Olympic gold with Team Canada in Salt Lake City. In 2006 in Turin, in her final Olympic Games, Goyette was given the honour of being Canada's flag bearer at the opening ceremonies. The women's team won their second Olympic gold medal at these Games.

Goyette was named head coach of the University of Calgary Dinos Varsity women's hockey team in 2007, meaning she would continue her hockey career as a coach at the Olympic Oval. She retired as a player in 2008. In 2013, she became only the third woman to be inducted into the International Ice Hockey Hall of Fame and was selected as assistant coach for the Canadian national women's team heading to Sochi, Russia for the 2014 Winter Olympic Games.

Collaborative Innovation

The Olympic Oval and its stakeholders have always been leaders in technology, providing resources and facilities for individuals who work to push the limits in sport research.

Wind Tunnels and Skin Suit Technology

Prior to the 2002 Salt Lake City Winter Olympics, researchers at the National Research Council (NRC) Canada Institute for Aerospace Research in Ottawa studied the effects of wind on athletes and their equipment, clothing and positioning. Scientists monitored athletes in a wind tunnel to test the aerodynamics of their body position and how their equipment was affecting their speed. The simulated speed of the wind tunnel was 125 km an hour, enabling the athletes to experiment with body position without fear of falling.

Long Track Technology

In 1999, Sport Scientist Consultant Dale Taylor began research on unique timing and training systems which would pinpoint long track training variables while skaters were on the ice. This system had the potential to enhance the long track program through testing of athletes and subsequent training modifications.

Skatebots

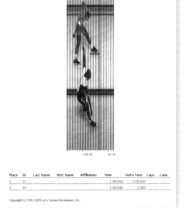

The University of Calgary's Skatebot event pitted autonomous robots against each other on the 400-metre Olympic Oval track. The bots were constructed by U of C engineering students from electric motors, programmable logic controllers and Lego Mindstorm pieces. The students chose to move the bots around the ice in various ways, some crude and clumsy, some with finesse, mimicking motions of the human skater. Dr. Daryl Caswell and Dr. Clifton Johnston developed the exercise for their first year engineering class to stress the importance of flexible thinking. The event was also designed to provide a cross-platform to integrate knowledge between faculties on campus such as engineering, art and kinesiology.

Fun Fact

Skaters at the Olympic Oval were some of the first to mold their speed skate boots to their feet, and bend their long track skate blades for increased performance—a common practice in short track but considered crazy for long track at the time. Bending the blade provides increased stability and turning capacity in the corners.

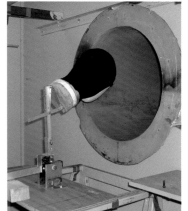

Short Track Safety Systems

In the early 1990s, research began into creating a safety mat system for the short track rink. Always focused on increasing performance and safety for the athletes, the Olympic Oval was the first speed skating oval to have padding in the corners on the 400-metre track. The padding around the long track ice had recently been heightened due to the increase in speed resulting from the introduction of the klap skate.

The impetus for creating a safer short track rink came when Shawn Holman, an Oval Program athlete, broke his femur in the middle of the 1992-1993 season. It was a serious accident which confirmed the need to create a system to protect the skaters.

To address the issue, Oval General Manager Jacques Thibault, Geoff Elliott, Mark Messer and Hugh Hamilton devised the first design for a boardless short track crash pad system on a napkin over lunch one day. The Faculty of Kinesiology assisted to develop and test

the prototype of the first boardless pad system which was installed around the north rink during the 1999-2000 season.

The international community was slow to accept the boardless crash pad system for short track. Even though there had been a system in place at the Olympic Oval since the year 2000, other facilities did not embrace the idea. The second generation of crash pads did not come to fruition until shortly before the Vancouver Winter Olympics in 2010.

Prior to these Olympics, the new pads were installed in Calgary and then taken to Salt Lake City and Beijing and were subsequently installed in Montreal. In Canada, national team trials only occur in facilities with boardless systems. There is still no international standard for crash pads in short track speed skating, but the model for safety has been set by this leading-edge pad system designed at the Olympic Oval, University of Calgary.

Changing the Way
Speed Skaters Coast

The Oval pioneered safety standards for long track speed skaters by requiring athletes and coaches to use the inside not the outside lane for cooling down after races and for coaches providing post-race feedback. Marcel Lacroix had been requesting this change for years, and Mark Greenwald eventually gave the task to Stacey Polet to make it happen after Cindy Klassen was injured on the outside lane. Enforcing a no-stopping zone in the outside lane was not an easy task, but it is now the norm at ovals around the world.

A Fashion Xplosion

As speed skating skin suit technology advances so does the fashion – allowing athletes to show off their unique style.

Derrick Campbell

Olympic Oval Wall of Champions Inductee 2003

Derrick came to the Olympic Oval in 1992 with a small group of short track skaters who were inspired by the idea of establishing a national short track training centre in western Canada. Until that time, the hub of short track speed skating was firmly in Montreal. Campbell was part of a core group of about a dozen athletes who made the journey west, somewhat on blind faith, but also with the support of Speed Skating Canada to develop a program at the Olympic Oval.

This small seed program quickly became a very competitive centre, with the group size growing as the program progressed. The program's innovative training model brought in ideas from other sports, including training protocols already developed in the long track program. International athletes also joined the Canadian skaters and soon the western national training centre was producing medal winners.

Derrick Campbell realized his full potential as a short track speed skater at the Olympic Oval and had his best results while training at the facility. He competed in two Winter Olympic Games, and was the first short track speed skater from the western training centre to win an Olympic gold medal when he reached the podium as a member of the 1998 Canadian men's 5000-metre relay team. He also won seven World Championship medals. As a tribute to his pursuit of excellence his banner was inducted onto the Olympic Oval Wall of Champions in 2003. He was the first short track speed skater to receive this honour at the facility.

Once retired from speed skating in 2000, Derrick transitioned from high performance athlete to coach — first, coaching in the Oval program; then the American short track squad in Turin, Italy for the 2006 Games. He then donned the red and white once again for the 2010 Vancouver Olympics as the coach of the men's short track relay team. They captured the silver medal for Canada in the men's 5000-metre relay.

Career Highlights

- 2-time Petro-Canada Coaching Excellence Award winner
- Inducted into the Cambridge, Ontario Sports Hall of Fame
- Olympic medal, gold
- Olympic Oval Wall of Champions Inductee
- Québec Coach of the Year
- Speed Skating Canada Coach of the Year

The Oval Office

At the core of the Olympic Oval's successes are the people who have poured their hearts and souls into day-to-day operations.

Over the past 25 years many have contributed time and energy to the Best Ever legacy venue. Some have moved on to other pursuits, but their energy and passion lives on.

Fun Fact

Many Oval Program athletes have had part-time jobs at the facility to help offset training costs. These jobs vary and include: guest services, weight room attendant, ice technicians, caretaking, administration, and summer camp coaches and coordinators. Some of these athletes have moved on to full-time positions and careers at the Oval.

Vision   *Together with our partners, we will drive the mission of Canadian athlete podium performances.*

Mission   *The Olympic Oval is a world class speed skating and high performance sport facility dedicated to the pursuit of excellence and health and wellness for all.*

"...a lot of times you can skate a personal best here... sometimes that means a world record...and it's great to get in front of a home crowd..."

– Jeremy Wotherspoon

Top of the World

XIX Olympic Winter Games, Salt Lake City, Utah, USA – February 8-24, 2002

Canadian speed skaters brought home another nine medals – three in long track events and six in short track.

The Olympic Oval trained women were the standout skaters at these Olympics. Catriona Le May Doan proudly carried the flag into the Salt Lake Olympic stadium at the Opening Cermonies, being given the honour after her double Olympic medal performance in Nagano (where she also carried the flag for the closing ceremonies). She overcame the so-called "curse of the Canadian team flag bearer" to win her third Olympic medal (and second Olympic gold) in the women's 500-metre at the 2002 Games.

Teammates Cindy Klassen and Clara Hughes both won bronze in the women's 3000-metre and women's 5000-metre distances respectively. This was also the last Olympic Games appearance for champions Susan Auch and Catorina Le May Doan, who both retired shortly after.

On the short track stage, Alanna Kraus-Handley lived up to expectations and won her first Olympic medal as part of the bronze medal winning 3000-metre women's relay team. Kraus-Handley also recorded top 10 finishes in the women's 500, 1000 and 1500-metre events.

Olympic Canadian National Team Coaches

The Olympic Oval also contributed a vast pool of talent to the Canadian team's coaching staff for the Salt Lake Winter Olympics. Derrick Auch, Moira D'Andrea, Sean Ireland, Mike Marshall, and Xiuli Wang were all part of the elite coaching contingent that travelled to Salt Lake.

Three of the five Olympic Oval coaches had family members competing in the Games. Sean Ireland coached his brother Mike to place in the top 10 in the men's 500-metre race. Derrick Auch, the brother of Susan Auch, and Mike Marshall, brother of Kevin

Marshall, both coached at the Salt Lake Games. Neal Marshall, the third Marshall brother and former Canadian Olympic speed skater was also in Salt Lake as a CBC Olympic analyst covering both short and long track speed skating.

The Olympic Oval high performance training program took centre stage in other country performances as well, as Oval-trained American Casey FitzRandolph gained notoriety for his gold medal performance on home soil.

Oval Trained Athletes in Salt Lake City

- **Speed Skating:** Susan Auch, Steven Elm, Kristina Groves, Clara Hughes, Mike Ireland, Cindy Klassen, Mark Knoll, Catriona Le May Doan, Kevin Marshall, Dustin Molicki, Cindy Overland, Jeremy Wotherspoon

- **Short Track :** Alanna Kraus-Handley

- **Women's Hockey:** Dana Antal, Kelly Bechard, Cassie Campbell, Lori Dupuis, Danielle Goyette, Cherie Piper, Colleen Sostorics, Hayley Wickenheiser

Along with these Canadian Olympians many athletes, coaches and support staff called the Oval home prior to participating in these Olympics.

Jeremy Wotherspoon

Olympic Oval Wall of Champions Inductee 2012

Jeremy is considered by many as the best speed skater of all time. With an impressive tally of victories, including 67 world cup wins, 19 World Championship medals and 17 world records it is difficult to argue. He is a 13-time world cup overall champion in the 500 and 1000-metre distances and has won four World Sprint Championship titles. He was inducted into the Speed Skating Canada Hall of Fame in 1998, Canada's Sports Hall of Fame in 2012, Olympic Oval Wall of Champions in 2012, and the Alberta Sport Hall of Fame in 2013.

Jeremy began skating at the Olympic Oval at the age of 8, travelling from his home in Red Deer, Alberta to train at the indoor venue. In the beginning, he skated in both short track and long track disciplines, but eventually specialized in long track, excelling in the sprint distances. He started training with the Canadian national team when he was 18.

At the age of 20 he burst on to the international scene, winning three 500-metre races and one 1000-metre race at the first two world cup events of the season. In that season he broke two world records, which began an unprecedented line of track and world records for Wotherspoon. The first world record came in November of 1997 in the sprint combination at the World Cup for Ladies and Men – Sprints and the second in the 1000-metre in December at the Canadian Single Distance Championships.

Wotherspoon's results only climbed from there. He continued to break world records, many of these set on home ice at the Oval, The Fastest Ice in the World™. He won his first World Sprint Championship title in 1999, and brought home subsequent titles in 2000, 2002 and 2003.

Olympic successes did not mirror Wotherspoon's dominance of the sport of speed skating. He won his only Olympic medal, a silver, in the 500-metre event at the Nagano Games in 1998. He was the favourite to win gold at these same Games in the 1000-metre race, but did not clinch a podium performance.

His struggles at the Olympics continued in Salt Lake in 2002, when he fell early in the 500-metre race. For his second 500-metre race at these Games he skated the fastest time of any of the competitors, but due to his fall he was unable to reach the podium. He was also not able to find success in Turin.

In 2007, Jeremy took a brief sabbatical from skating. He returned the next season with a world record performance at the first world cup event of the year. At the 2010 Games he finished 9th in the 500-metre and 14th overall in the 1000-metre distance. After Vancouver, he announced his retirement and subsequently went to coach at the new training centre in Inzell, Germany.

At the 2012 Essent ISU World Sprint Speed Skating Championships at the Olympic Oval (Jan. 28-29, 2012), a tribute was held for Wotherspoon, and his banner was raised to the Olympic Oval Wall of Champions alongside fellow speed skaters Susan Auch, Catriona Le May Doan, Kevin Crockett and Derrick Campbell.

Veteran sports broadcaster Steve Armitage emceed the ceremony. Jeremy's wife and former national team member Kim Weger, his daughter Ella, his parents, sisters, former teammates, coaches and representatives from Speed Skating Canada and the Olympic Oval stood alongside him as he accepted the honour. Fans, supporters and friends in the stands also looked on as the banner was unveiled on the second corner of the 400-metre oval.

As he accepted his award, Jeremy noted, "It is a great feeling to be honoured for what I have done in speed skating, especially in Calgary, the home of Canadian speed skating. If not for the Olympic Oval, not only would we have no walls on which to honour Canadian Olympic medallists, but there is a good chance there would be no posters to put up. This facility has changed the face of speed skating in Canada, and I am very thankful to be honoured at the facility that I am so indebted to."

In June of 2013, Jeremy Wotherspoon announced he was coming out of retirement with the goal of qualifying for the 2014 Winter Olympic Games in Sochi, Russia.

Fun Fact
Jeremy Wotherspoon was a past winner at the Olympic Oval Top Blade Camp, demonstrating that many of the skaters enrolled in these camps go on to become elite athletes later on in their speed skating careers.

Career Highlights

- 9-time Speed Skating Canada Male Skater of the Year Long Track (this award was renamed the Jeremy Wotherspoon Award)
- 10 junior world records (all at the Oval)
- 17 senior world records
- 67 world cup victories
- Alberta Sport Hall of Fame Inductee
- Canada's Sports Hall of Fame Inductee
- Gagne Family Award, Wotherspoon family
- Olympic medal, silver
- Olympic Oval Wall of Champions Inductee
- Oscar Mathisen Award
- Scott Mamini Memorial Award for Male Athlete of the Year, Calgary Booster Club
- Speed Skating Canada Hall of Fame Inductee

Skating Camps

Early on, coaches and staff identified a need to provide speed skating instruction through seasonal camps and short term programs.

These camps would serve a number of purposes. They would build a framework to develop young speed skaters, who would ideally go on to compete at the elite level, and allow development opportunities for older elite skaters to improve their skills. They would provide the opportunity for school-aged children to skate at a recreational level and learn about the sport of speed skating. Finally, some camps gave employment mentorship and coach training to older, experienced skaters, teaching them how to break down skills and give back to the next generation.

The first summer speed skating camps were held in July of 1989 and were led by Jack Walters, Oval coach and former U.S. Olympic speed skating team member.

There were two instructional camps open to local, national and international skaters. They were for serious skaters with several years of experience who wanted to develop a better understanding of speed skating technique and training. The camps lasted five and a half days, starting Monday and ending Saturday afternoon.

In addition to the skating and dryland training, the camps included classroom instruction. A broad range of topics were covered off-ice, from skating mechanics and racing skills, to video analysis of the 1988 Olympic Games.

School Program

The year after the Calgary Olympics, the Oval started a grassroots school program. The objective was to integrate speed skating into schools as a physical education activity and introduce the sport to children as a potential life-long and possibly competitive activity. It was also an initiative designed to grow the sport from the ground up.

Experienced coaches ran the on and off-ice curriculum, which included: long track and short track training, equipment care and maintenance, speed skating history, and dryland training.

Oval Program
Short Track Attitude Camp

This extremely challenging camp was started by coaches Andrew Barron and Marcel Lacroix and ran from approximately 1995 to 1998. The camp featured extreme back country camping and hiking with a guide, mountain biking, and hap-ki-do, in addition to on-ice training.

Summer Speed
High Performance Camp

The Summer Speed High Performance Camp started in 1996 to provide provincial club level skaters the opportunity to train in a consistent setting early in the season. The camp was designed to expose the best of Canada's provincial skaters to training programs at the Olympic Oval.

Summer Speed is still offered every summer. It includes long track and short track streams and skaters attending the camp participate in both disciplines. Participants range in age from 5 to 18, and come from every province and territory in the country. International skaters also attend, with the bulk coming from the United States. Skaters are members of provincial/territorial/state speed skating organizations who intend to follow a competitive, elite-level speed skating path.

Summer Speed is a great opportunity for young athletes to improve their on-ice and off-ice technical skills. These attendees often transition to full time Oval Program skaters in the years following their summer camp experiences.

Top Blade
High Performance Camp

Top Blade High Performance Camp got its name from the movie "Top Gun" – bringing together "the best of the best". The Oval offers this camp for both short track and long track disciplines. These are high intensity camps with sessions on and off the ice, including training at high altitude through mountain hikes.

Masters Speed
High Performance Camp

Started in 1998, the Masters Speed High Performance Camp is a long track speed skating development program for adult speed skaters. It is a chance for skaters over the age of 35 to experience the elite training environment of the Olympic Oval and skate on the Fastest Ice in the World™. The skaters attending these camps are by no means recreational or beginner level, but high-level club skaters focused on improving their athletic performance and technical skills.

Absolute Speed Camp

The inaugural Absolute Speed Camp was held in February 1998, in conjunction with the 1998 Olympic Games. This camp introduces beginner level youth and adult skaters to the sport of speed skating. The camp emerged as a response to demand and interest in speed skating after the outstanding success of Canadian speed skaters on the international stage, and in anticipation of the results at the Nagano Games.

Power Skating Camp

The Oval's Power Skating Camp was introduced in 2009, and is targeted towards young hockey and ringette players. It helps players develop speed skating skills that complement their game play and improve their stride, agility, balance and coordination. Instructors in this program are current Oval Program and national team speed skaters who were past elite hockey players.

Fun Facts

- Top Blade and Summer Speed camps culminate with exciting races, allowing participants to practice skills in a competition setting.

- Top Blade Camp winners have included speed skating stars such as Apolo Ohno and Jeremy Wotherspoon.

- Absolute Speed Camp was later adopted by the Calgary Speed Skating Association as a recruitment program for their club.

Going Out with a Bang

Personal Best Times Fall at Finale

Each racing season culminates with the Oval Finale. Athletes from all over the world are drawn to Calgary to race in the Olympic Oval's largest competition of the year. It is open to all ISU-registered competitive speed skaters in both junior and senior categories. Pairings are based on personal best times and there is no limit to the number of competitors per country, or to which categories they race in. These pairings over the years have produced unique combinations and exciting races. Prizes are awarded for personal bests, national country records and world records. The first Olympic Oval Finale was held in 1991. Gregor Jelonek, Susan Auch, Michelle Morton and Mike Marshall were among the Canadian competitors.

Finale was created because the staff at the Oval wanted to grow speed skating at the grassroots level. They decided the best way to do this was to hold a competition that brought together young, emerging talent and the world's top skaters. They hoped this unique competition format would motivate the young skaters. It worked! Finale continued to grow, and in 2012 was the largest ever, with 14 countries participating and 100 pairs for the men's 500-metre distance.

In the early days, volunteers and staff would sit in the Oval lounge or on the timing deck until the wee hours of the morning and document the world records in triplicate, by hand, on huge spreadsheets. No corrections were allowed on the final sheets (no erasing, no whiteout) and the statistics had to include the lap times as well. If a mistake was made anywhere in the process, the entire spreadsheet had to be redone. If an error happened on a 10,000-metre race or on the last entry of an event, the despair heard from the statisticians echoed throughout the university campus.

The long hours and hard work Oval staff and volunteers put into this internationally acclaimed event are enormous. Finale has a reputation for being high-spirited and creating a fun atmosphere in which to race. A long-standing tradition during the event is the creation of clever poems that are printed on slips of paper and left secretly on staff desks each day of the event. There is always a sweet treat to accompany the creative prose!

Day 6 – Oval Finale
Final Day of Competition

*Oval Finale is here, it's our challenge, our mission,
to host the best ever and largest competition!*

*The Olympic Oval with all our staff and
friends is truly an amazing place,*

*skaters come from far and wide
to have their fastest race!*

*So here is a treat for a little pick
me up on our final day,*

*let's do it for the skaters with
one last hip hip hooray!*

Patrick Seltsam

American speed skater Patrick Seltsam competed in every Finale from 1991 to 2008. He missed 2009 because he was working the World Figure Skating Championships in Los Angeles. He generally raced the 500-metre and his goal was for his time in seconds to be close to his age at the time.

Bonnie Blair Retires

Bonnie Blair celebrated her 31st birthday on March 18, 1995 at the Olympic Oval during the Oval Finale competition. The next day, she laced up her skates for the last time. This was her last day of competitive speed skating and her last lap around the rink that had meant so much to her over her lifetime as a competitive athlete.

Racing beside her was Susan Auch, who for this Finale competition would again challenge Blair in the 500-metre sprint. The past repeated itself with Blair winning in another one-two finish. Blair won the 1000-metre category too, ending her career on a high. As always Blair's mother Eleanor and the rest of the Blair clan were in the stands to support her, along with the Oval family that was a constant throughout the years.

Long Running Competitions

In addition to the competitions run by the Organizing Committee Calgary on behalf of Speed Skating Canada, the Olympic Oval also organizes numerous local, national and international speed skating competitions each year.

These annual, long running competitions give skaters from around the world a chance to compete in a high performance environment and achieve personal bests. These competitions also bring athletes together to foster a strong speed skating community where participants, officials and volunteers build memories and share achievements. Through these events, Canadian, provincial and club athletes also compete with home soil advantage.

Fun Facts

• *Sport plays a significant role in the Calgary economy, providing a boost to the tourism industry. Besides visitor spending during speed skating competitions, an added benefit comes from national and international exposure of the events through broadcast, print and online media. Oval events are covered in various countries besides Canada, including the USA, The Netherlands, Germany, China and Japan.*

• *The Olympic Oval hosts approximately 50 speed skating competitions each season.*

Long Track

• **Oval Finale*** (International Event)
• **CanAm*** (International Event)
• **Oval Invitational*** (International Event)
• **Summer Classic – Single Distance Competition*** (International Event)
• **Fall Classic – Single Distance Competition*** (International Event)
• **Alberta Open**** (Western Canadian Ability Level Event)
• **Saturday Morning Races/Time Trials** (training races for high performance athletes, including provincial, national and international skaters)

Short Track

• **Oktoberfest**** (depending on schedules is sometimes an international event)
• **Winterfest**** (Canadian Sanctioned Event)
• **RU Fast**** (Western Canadian Ability Level Event)
• **Single Distance Series** (provincial level athletes race to secure qualifying times for national age class competitions, trials and championships).

Categories

***International Event** – Athletes race to meet qualifying times for major international events (i.e. world cups, World Championships, Olympic Games).

****Canadian Sanctioned Event** – Provincial and team level athletes compete to achieve qualifying times.

*****Western Canadian Ability Level Event** – Hosted by Alberta Amateur Speed Skating Association (AASSA) and the Calgary Speed Skating Association (CSSA), supported by the Olympic Oval.

Volunteers

Without the energy of the volunteers that have been involved with the Olympic Oval since the beginning, the competitions and programs at the facility could not run.

Oval volunteers come from all walks of life, but share a love of speed skating and, more fundamentally, a love of the Oval. Some came to volunteer after seeing the pre-Olympic event prior to the 1988 Olympic Winter Games, others came to the building through encounters with coaches and athletes who raved about the facility, and still others from their children's involvement in the sport of speed skating. The Olympic Oval's long-time volunteers all speak highly of the support of the staff and athletes they have met along the way.

In Their Words ...

"I got involved in volunteering at the Oval with speed skating in the fall of 2006 when I met a development coach at a Living Well exercise program...I was put to work counting laps and have been doing it ever since. I have since had the opportunity to volunteer at the Vancouver 2010 Winter Olympics as a lap recorder. I have also had the opportunity to meet athletes from different countries. I am now a level 3 accredited Lap Recorder."

– Richard

"During the year 2000 I was thinking about what else I would want to do when I retired...I volunteered, was assigned as a timer and have been doing it ever since. I find all Oval staff truly appreciate the efforts of volunteers...Helping at the Oval is fun, and we get to watch dedicated athletes develop in front of us year after year."

– Hugh

"My 'accidental' introduction to speed skating resulted from volunteering as a first aid attendant during the BC Winter Games, where I was assigned to short track speed skating. I was so impressed with the drive, determination and utter fearlessness of the young skaters, when I moved to Calgary I decided to volunteer at the Oval...Over the years my Oval volunteer journey has led to certification as a technical official, the enjoyment of volunteering at numerous world cups and even participating as a technical official at the Vancouver 2010 Winter Olympics. Without the great group of Oval volunteers, the incredible Oval staff and the privilege of being an integral part of many a young skater's journey as they strive to become elite athletes, I would never have had the opportunity for these great life experiences."

– Brad

"...In 1987 my family attended the pre-Olympic speed skating world cup where I was in awe of the facility and the sport of speed skating. After that event, our son Michael decided he was going to be a speed skater...and my volunteering began...I continue to volunteer because of the welcoming feeling I get when I enter the Oval...There are very few sports where you can mingle and talk to top athletes and Olympians. It is a friendly, supportive sport and the Olympic Oval made it available to everyone. WE are so fortunate to have the Olympic Oval in our city."

– Shirley

"...I became involved...at the Oval, when my son moved over from Saskatoon to become involved with the high performance speed skating team back in 1998. I have had the pleasure to work many, many meets at the Oval since then, including ISU World Championships and world cups as well as SSC national and AASSA events. I love being in the action at ice-level and will continue to support events at the Oval for many years to come. The Oval is an amazing facility and the volunteers who work, they are wonderful, fun folks."

– Dave

"When the Oval was built prior to the 1988 Winter Olympics, I was working for the vice-president in charge of the University of Calgary construction for the Games. I came to know how special the facility would be...A few years after the Olympics, the Oval sent a message around campus asking if anyone would be willing to take in a speed skater, as they came from all over the world to train in Calgary. I had a young female speed skater from Regina living with me for two years and at the end of that time...I was hooked and offered to volunteer...Going into my 18th season as a volunteer official, I have no inclination to stop supporting our wonderful athletes. Speed skating is a huge part of my life and hopefully will be for years to come."

– Gloria

Olympic Oval Gala

The Olympic Oval Gala started in 2005 to support the bursary fund and the Olympic Oval high performance sport programs.

05 The Olympic Oval Athlete Bursary Fund was established recognizing the financial burden Canadian athletes experience training at a high performance level. The idea behind the fund was to financially support the athletic careers of Canadian Olympic Oval speed skaters and assist with competition travel fees, purchasing new training equipment, paying for food and rent. Since the fund was established, many athletes have applied and 40 athletes have received cheques from the fund.

The United Farmers' of Alberta was the first presenting sponsor of the Gala, which was held as a Stampede Party at the Red and White Club at McMahon Stadium (formerly the Calgary '88 Volunteer Centre). Attendees were given the chance to kick up their heels, mix and mingle with Oval Program athletes and coaches at this inaugural event.

Over the years, the Olympic Oval Gala has had a number of themes and venues, all designed to promote a fun and festive atmosphere to support the Oval Programs. In 2007 the Gala was moved to the Olympic Oval itself and branded as a pre-Stampede party.

In conjunction with the 25th Anniversary celebrations, the 2012 theme celebrated the success of the Oval's Calgary '88 Olympic legacy. Six of Calgary's top chefs were enlisted to create Winter Olympic host country themed food, opening Canada Olympic Park's Markin MacPhail Centre.

The community's generosity in supporting the Oval Gala over the years has gone a long way in assisting Oval High Performance Program athletes in their pursuit of excellence. To date, the event has raised approximately $200,000 for the bursary fund and Oval athletes.

Kevin Crockett

Olympic Oval Wall of Champions Inductee 2005

Kevin was a member of the Canadian national long track team that competed at the 1998 Nagano Winter Games. During these Games he won a bronze in the 500-metre event, one of four Canadian long track speed skaters to medal. Prior to these Olympics, Crockett set the world record in the both the 1000-metre (Dec. 23, 1995) and 1500-metre (Nov. 29, 1997) on home ice at the Calgary Olympic Oval. During the 1997-1998 season he also won seven medals at world cup competitions.

His podium performance in Nagano was the realization of a long-held Olympic dream for Crockett, and a recovery from the disappointment of not being able to compete at the Lillehammer Winter Olympics four years prior. While training for the 1994 Games, Kevin was in a car accident which affected his ability to perform at the national team trials.

In 2002, Crockett retired from competitive speed skating to follow in his father's footsteps as a coach (Crockett is the brother of speed skaters Amanda and Cindy Overland – both Olympic competitors who also trained at the Olympic Oval – and the son of speed skater and coach Ernie Overland). He quickly found his place, flourishing in the Olympic Oval high performance program, coaching skaters from Canada, China, Japan and Greece. Most notably, he coached Chinese speed skater Beixing Wang to a series of successful finishes, including a bronze medal at the 2010 Vancouver Olympics and a first place finish at the World Sprint Championships in Moscow in 2009.

A key factor in Crockett's coaching method was a direct result of his time spent at the Oval as an athlete and influenced by his former coach Jack Walters and others at the facility. Early in his speed skating career he was introduced to high-altitude training, working under the guidance of Walters and University of Calgary Exercise and Health Physiologist Dr. David Smith. Smith had been working on research designed to maximize athlete performances using high-altitude training. Following this research protocol, every summer, Crockett would take his athletes away from the rink for some high-altitude training in the Rocky Mountains.

Kevin Crockett was inducted into the Cambridge Sports Hall of Fame in 1997, an honour also given to fellow speed skater, Oval alumni, Derrick Campbell and Olympic Oval Associate Director Shawn Holman. Kevin's banner was raised to the Olympic Oval Wall of Champions in January 2005 at the Essent ISU World Cup Speed Skating.

Kevin Crockett Career Highlights

- 7-time world cup medallist
- Olympic medal, bronze
- Olympic Oval Wall of Champions Inductee
- World record, 1000-metre and 1500-metre

Coaching Excellence

Throughout its 25 year history, the Olympic Oval has fostered excellence in coaching through innovative programs and a cross-disciplinary approach.

Coaches at the facility are exposed to state-of-the-art resources (including sports medicine) and have opportunities to share and discuss coaching methods with like-minded coaches involved in other sports. The Oval programs – speed skating, cycling and women's hockey – have produced a long list of World Champions and Olympic medallists. Coaches have also won numerous awards of excellence over the years in their respective sports.

Through the National Coaching Institute (NCI), professional development symposiums and a facility-wide dedication to innovation, Olympic Oval coaches have reached the level of some of the best in the world.

Following participation in the 1992 Olympics in Albertville, Mark Greenwald made his way north. After a brief club coaching role in British Columbia, he returned to Calgary in 1993 and took a job with the Olympic Oval under program manager Jacques Thibault as a coach and coordinator of the Oval Program – Open Class. Mark spent his early years at the Oval developing the foundation for this novel initiative that would eventually join with the Olympic Oval High Performance Speed Skating Program.

After 12 years in Calgary coaching and leading the Oval's four athlete programs to a long series of Olympic and world titles, Greenwald was appointed as the first ever Director of the Olympic Oval.

Mark Greenwald

As director, Greenwald succeeded in building on the already successful Oval programs, doubling coaching staff from 12 to 25 in a few short years and increasing program registration. This period in history saw the Olympic Oval's dominance on the world stage realized.

Oval Long Track Coaches over the Years

- Derrick Auch
- Andrew Barron
- Kevin Crockett
- Moira D'Andrea
- Abby Ennis
- Mark Greenwald
- Arno Hoogveld
- Bill Hoyne
- Kurt Innes
- Mike Ireland

- Sean Ireland
- Matt Jordan
- Jeff Kitura
- Marcel Lacroix
- Neal Marshall
- Mike Marshall
- Todd McClements
- Gregg Planert
- Crispin Parkinson
- Ingrid Paul

- Jean Pichette
- Chris Shelley
- Jacques Thibault
- Jack Walters
- Mark Wild
- Xiuli Wang
- Jeremy Wotherspoon

Oval Short Track Coaches over the Years

- Andrew Barron
- Derrick Campbell
- Jon Cavar
- Yvon Deblois
- Janos Englert
- Debby Fisher
- Shawn Holman
- Marcel Lacroix
- Tony Main
- Alan McIlveen
- Miwako Muraoka
- Maggie Qi
- Ayako Tsubaki

2006

"The goal in 2006 was to exceed the success in 2002. Things just clicked!"

– Cindy Klassen

Canada's Medal Factory

XX Olympic Winter Games, Turin, Italy – February 10-26, 2006

In Turin, Canada placed third overall in medal count with a total of 24 medals, behind only Germany (29 medals) and the United States (25 medals) .

 06 Cindy Klassen, Clara Hughes and Kristina Groves, were the story of these Games, finishing top in the medal count with nine medals between them. Cindy Klassen's record five medal performance is still unmatched in Canada's history in the sport. Clara Hughes and Kristina Groves both won individual medals – Hughes a gold in the 5000-metre and Groves a silver in the 1500-metre distance. Together the trio of Klassen, Groves and Hughes took home a silver medal in the women's Team Pursuit event.

The men's long track pursuit team of Arne Dankers, Steven Elm, and Denny Morrison also took home a silver medal in their event, finishing second to underdog Italians in the Team Pursuit final. Justin Warsylewicz, the youngest member of the Canadian Olympic team at the time, and Jason Parker also both won silver as alternates on the pursuit squad. The Torino Olympics were the first Winter Games to feature the Team Pursuit events for both men and women, making Canada's medals even more special.

On the short track, Alanna Kraus-Handley continued her Olympic medal winning ways with a silver as part of the women's team that placed second in the 3000-metre relay.

All of these skaters lived and trained in Calgary, and their homecoming to the Oval

was an Olympic-sized party, with bronze, silver and gold medals on display for a crowd of excited and adoring fans.

The Oval (and Canada's) medals did not end with speed skating, however, with other Calgary-based athletes capturing the heart of the nation at the Games. Ex-speed skater Duff Gibson won Canada's first Winter Olympic gold medal in skeleton. Gibson began his career in high performance sports as a rower, moved on to speed skating, then bobsleigh, and finally skeleton where he reached his goal of Olympic champion in 2006. His win was one of the emotional highlights of the Games as it closely followed the death of his father, who lost his 11-year battle with cancer shortly before Torino.

Oval Trained Athletes at Torino

- **Speed Skating:** Arne Dankers, Steven Elm, Kristina Groves, Clara Hughes, Mike Ireland, Cindy Klassen, Brock Miron, Denny Morrison, Krisy Myers, Christine Nesbitt, Jason Parker, Shannon Rempel, Kerry Simpson, Justin Warsylewicz, Kim Weger, Jeremy Wotherspoon

- **Short Track:** Alanna Kraus-Handley

- **Women's Hockey:** Cassie Campbell, Gillian Ferrari, Danielle Goyette, Gina Kingsbury, Carla MacLeod, Cherie Piper, Colleen Sostorics, Hayley Wickenheiser

Along with these Canadian Olympians many athletes, coaches and support staff called the Oval home prior to participating in these Olympics.

Fun Fact

Ice-meister Mark Messer buried a gold maple leaf in the ice at the Torino speed skating oval to give Canadian speed skaters an edge, following in the footsteps of Trent Evans who had secretly buried a loonie at centre ice for the hockey tournament in Salt Lake City. Messer pulled the maple leaf out of the ice after Clara Hughes won her gold medal in the 5000-metre event.

Cindy Klassen

Six-time Olympic Medallist

Cindy has won six Olympic medals, and shares the title of Canada's most decorated Olympian with fellow speed skater Clara Hughes. She is the only Canadian Olympian and first female speed skater to win five medals in a single Olympic Games at the 2006 Winter Olympics in Turin. Her sixth medal was won at the previous Winter Olympics in 2002 in Salt Lake City, where she was coached by Moira d'Andrea.

Originally from Winnipeg, Manitoba, her speed skating hero was fellow Olympic medallist and Oval trained skater Susan Auch. As a child, Cindy excelled in a number of sports and competed for Canada on the international stage in field lacrosse (1994 Commonwealth Games), women's hockey (1996 member of national junior women's hockey team), and in-line skating (1999 PanAm Games). She reluctantly tried speed skating on her parent's suggestion, and recalls kids flying past her at her first practice. But, by the end of her first year, Manitoba provincial coach Anne Mushumanski encouraged Cindy to train hard to qualify for the Canada Games (which she accomplished) and then move to Calgary to further her speed skating career. Cindy relocated to Calgary the following season in 1999 and qualified for the junior national team in her first season.

Neal Marshall coached Cindy from 2002 to 2007, and at the Torino Winter Olympics. Klassen excelled under Marshall's program. She gives him, along with all of her coaches throughout her career, huge credit for her phenomenal successes. To Klassen, who was a "workhorse" skater, Marshall was the perfect coach at the right time. He

provided her with the confidence to be a fierce competitor. A great speed skater in his own right, he was strong in the same distances as Klassen (he set a world record in the 1500-metre race during his skating career) and brought this experience to her.

In 2008, Cindy faced a family crisis when her sister's car went off a bridge in Winnipeg into the Red River. Klassen was preparing for the World Championships in Germany at the time and she flew back to Canada to be with her family. She prayed to God for peace, putting her trust in His divine control and support. Her sister made an incredible recovery.

In preparation for the Vancouver 2010 Games, Klassen struggled to make the national team after undergoing bilateral knee surgery. She did not win a medal at these Games, but was thrilled to have competed in front of a home crowd. She was proud to be Canadian and honoured to be on the Olympic team for the third time in her career.

Cindy has indicated, providing she qualifies, her last Winter Olympics will be 2014 in Sochi. Canadians will once again rise to support their national athletes as they

go to the line to represent the maple leaf in Russia.

As her speed skating career winds down, Cindy reflects fondly on her training at the Olympic Oval, appreciative of the facility, the incredible ice conditions, and the Oval's connection to the University of Calgary. She feels very fortunate to train and compete with the support of the Oval family around her.

Fun Facts

• *Prior to moving to Calgary, Cindy Klassen competed at the inaugural CIAU Western Women's Hockey Championship tournament hosted by the U of C at the Olympic Oval, where she was named defensive MVP alongside Colleen Sostorics and forward Kelly Bechard (both soon to be Oval Program athletes and female hockey Olympic medallists). While in the penalty box during one of the games she discussed where to get a pair of speed skates with Oval ice-maker, speed skater and competition volunteer Marc McGee.*

• *The Royal Canadian Mint featured Cindy on a 2010 Canadian quarter as part of their Olympic Memories Collection.*

Career Highlights

- 2-time Bobbie Rosenfeld Canadian Sport Awards Female Athlete of the Year
- 2 World All-Round Speed Skating Championships overall title
- 4-time Speed Skating Canada Female Skater of the Year, Long Track
- 6 Olympic medals
- Canadian Team Flag Bearer Turin Winter Olympic closing ceremony
- Cindy Klassen Recreation Centre in Winnipeg named after her
- Lou Marsh Award as Canada's Athlete of the Year
- Order of Manitoba
- Oscar Mathisen Award

20th Anniversary

The Oval celebrated its 20th anniversary during the 2007-2008 season. The facility was busy with programs, competitions, community events and research all running at full speed.

07 The Oval long and short track programs had outstanding results and record personal bests set by Oval Program athletes. The facility hosted a total of 62 competitions and events, and the Olympic Oval Research Group supported a number of important projects, including: Vancouver 2010 crash pad design and testing, Own the Podium "Top Secret" projects, and Faculty of Kinesiology research and studies.

Outside of speed skating, the Olympic Oval Female Hockey Program and Olympic Oval National Cycling Centre both continued to train a record number of high performance athletes. The 20th anniversary season saw the Dinos women's hockey team join the Olympic Oval women's hockey program as the Varsity tier.

Olympic Oval Anneau olympique
1988-2008

As the celebration of two decades of excellence continued, one of the high-lights of the season was the ING Finale. On March 14, 2008, Oval skater Denny Morrison was awarded $25,000 in ING prize money for setting the world record in the 1500-metre a week after winning a gold medal at the World Championships in Nagano. He skated a time of 1.42.01, beating the old record held by Oval Program training partner Shani Davis of the USA. The Olympic Oval produced a half-hour

Fun Fact

The 20th anniversary marked the start of the Road to 2010 campaign, getting athletes, staff, and fans excited for the 2010 Olympics in Vancouver. The Oval branded a van to carry the message into the community.

highlight show of that year's Finale which aired later on TSN.

The total 20-year world record count on The Fastest Ice in the World™ at the end of the 2007-2008 season was 249 in long track speed skating and 24 in short track speed skating.

Alanna Kraus-Handley

Olympic Oval Wall of Champions Inductee 2012

Alanna was a member of the Canadian national short track team from 1998 to 2008, and competed for Canada at the both the 2002 Salt Lake City Winter Olympics and the 2006 Winter Games in Turin. She is a two-time Olympic medallist, winning bronze in 2002 in the 3000-metre relay and silver in 2006, also in the relay. She holds seven World Championship medals. Kraus-Handley started speed skating at the age of four in her home town of Abbotsford, British Columbia, and took to the sport immediately.

She suffered an Achilles tendon injury following her silver medal relay performance at the 2006 Winter Games in Turin, and took the rest of the 2006-2007 season off to heal. She returned to the ice in 2007-2008, skating under coaches Jon Cavar and Yvon Deblois.

As the 2007-2008 season started, Alanna had already expressed that she would retire before the 2010 Winter Olympics in Vancouver. She said she only wanted to skate one more year to prove that she could come back from her injury. True to her word, she retired in 2008.

Kraus-Handley is one of the most successful short track speed skaters to ever train at the Olympic Oval, and was inducted on to the Olympic Oval Wall of Champions on October 20, 2012 during the ISU World Cup Short Track event. Her banner hangs alongside fellow short track skater Derrick Campbell's, paying tribute to her outstanding career and Olympic successes.

Defying the Odds

Many athletes overcome physical and mental challenges to achieve personal bests. The Oval has seen many of these fierce competitors come through its doors.

Crystal Phillips

At the age of 19, on the crest of a promising speed skating career, Oval Program speed skater Crystal Phillips was diagnosed with Multiple Sclerosis. Instead of letting her disease take control of her life, she turned it into an opportunity – a chance to educate others about the illness, a chance to talk to young people about the power of positivity, and a chance to raise money for neurological research. She established the Branch Out Foundation (a charity whose mandate is to raise funds for research into natural, holistic therapies for neurological disorders), and continues to spread her message of hope and happiness throughout the speed skating community and beyond.

The Games   The Globe and Mail, Wednesday, Februar

SOUNDS OF SILENCE / *Short-tracker Chantale Sévigny hopes to hear the only thing she can — a few notes of the national anthem.*

Deaf skater defies odds

BY JAMES CHRISTIE
The Globe and Mail
Nagano

THE only thing Chantale Sévigny can hear is the only thing she wants to hear — a few notes of her national anthem played at the Olympics.

The 22-year-old alternate on the Canadian women's short-track speed-skating relay team lives in silence, except for a few vibrations transmitted by a device behind her left ear. A little bit of music is about all that gets through. A childhood disease left her deaf, but she is more defiant than disabled.

"Someone asked her if she felt like going to the Paralympics, and she glared with disbelief," said Marcel Lacroix, the coach who mouthed English questions in French for Sévigny to lip-read and who then translated her spoken answers. She said: "What do you think I am? I made the Olympic team. I made The Show. Would you ask Wayne Gretzky to play in Hamilton [in the American Hockey League]?"

The native of Sherbrooke, Que., fought more battles than most to get to the Olympic team, where she's the backup to Isabelle Charest, 27, of Montreal, Annie Perreault, 26, of Rock Forest, Que., Tania Vicent, 22, of Laval, Que., and Christine Boudrias, 25, of Montreal.

Sévigny, a former figure skater, began skating at eight years of age and as a child was in the same club as speed skater Sylvie Daigle, who was her inspiration. She climbed the ladder via local events, then through the Quebec Games and Canada Games to show she was strong enough for the national team. Four years ago, she watched the Olympic opening ceremony from Lillehammer on television and decided she wanted to be in the next one.

Two years ago, she faced a difficult decision. The national speed-skating team trains at the Olympic Oval in Calgary. To go there would mean leaving behind all the support of home — family, the skating community that understood and nurtured her and a francophone environment.

"She could read lips only in French," Lacroix said, "not a word of English. But Chantale had the guts to say, 'I'm going. I'll manage.'

"To my troops in Calgary, she's a role model. She doesn't make excuses. If she doesn't win, she says, 'I won't get beat that way again.' She doesn't point a finger at the world and say, 'I lost because I'm handicapped and she won because she's not.'

"Other kids would bitch and complain. This shy little girl just comes in and kicks butt. As a coach, this brings you back to life, back to earth."

Sévigny was the third-fastest 500-metre short tracker in Canada at the national championships but hasn't skated with the veterans on the relay team — hence her alternate status.

"We're not afraid to put her into the game: She's been skating in the international circus for a couple of years," Lacroix said. "Either way, this is a great experience for her for Salt Lake City in 2002."

The fact that Sévigny was able to make one of the top-ranked teams in her sport speaks volumes for her talent, observed Nathalie Lambert, a star of the 1992 and 1994 Olympic squads with a gold medal and two silvers to her credit.

"She's powerful at the start because the starter stands in front of the skaters and she can see the smoke from the pistol before a hearing skater would hear the sound," Lambert said. "But she had to develop her peripheral vision, because she can't hear another skater coming up to pass her."

Sévigny's eyes dart back and forth during a singles race as she looks for cues flashed by the coach. But in the rough confusion of a short-track relay race, the cues must come from screaming teammates on the ice, and there's no time to read lips.

"They don't have a way to communicate with her right now, and so it might handicap the team if she was a starter," said Lambert, who broke her ankle Nov. 12 and is here as both a broadcaster and newspaper reporter.

The women's relay team is one of the medal favourites, with three former Olympic medalists in Boudrias, Perreault and Charest, the world-record holder in the 500-metre sprint. If the national anthem is played, Sévigny will be there for it, whether she has competed or not. She'll feel the music, read the words on Canadian lips.

At an Olympics where Canada's experience has been tainted by bickering between French and English speakers, the young woman who hears the words of neither is a perfect antidote.

"A handicap should not come between you and your dream," she said.

Chantale Sévigny, an alternate on the Canadian women's short-track speed-skating team, was left deaf by a childhood disease, but she is more defiant than disabled.   *(Canadian Pre...)*

Chantale Sevigny

Calgary-based short track national team skater Chantale Sevigny qualified for the 1998 Olympic Games in Nagano. Chantal, deaf from birth, started speed skating at the age of eight, and went on to succeed despite having to overcome her disability. One of her biggest challenges while racing was hearing the starter's pistol and the lap bells. She relied on the sight of smoke from the starter gun and signals from her coach to find her position on the ice. As a francophone moving to Calgary, she also needed to learn how to lip read English.

Kevin Frost

The forty-year-old Canadian speed skater, suffering from Ushers Syndrome, competed at the 2007 World Masters International Speed Skating Games. His illness left him with 20% hearing and blind, but he competed with his guide dog Nemo close by to cheer him on.

World Masters

The Olympic Oval has hosted the World Masters Speed Skating Games twice since opening its doors in 1987.

07 From February 22-25, 2007, the 16th Annual Masters International Speed Skating Games welcomed 288 competitors (65 ladies, 223 men) to The Fastest Ice in the World™. These four-day games still hold the record for being the largest, and were the first to add an extra day to the competition, going from a three-day to four-day event. A total of 14 countries competed, including: Austria, Canada, Finland, Germany, Ireland, Italy, Latvia, The Netherlands, Norway, Romania, Russia, Switzerland, Ukraine, and the USA. The ice on this special weekend was perfect. Nearly all Masters International Records (IMSSC Records) that could be broken were broken during the competition—a total of 93 records were set.

The second time the competition was held at the Olympic Oval was in February of 2011. The 20th Annual World Masters International Speed Skating Games took place from February 24-27, 2011, with 222 skaters (52 ladies, 170 men) from 12 countries (Canada, Finland, Germany, Greece, Italy, Latvia, The Netherlands, Norway, Romania, Russia, Switzerland, and the USA).

Mastering Masters

Athletes Celebrate • In 2007, the participants were served up some western hospitality at a welcome banquet for the skaters on the first evening. A closing banquet with line dancing at Cowboys and an awards ceremony closed out the festivities.

Joe McDonald • Coming into this event having broken all records in his age class, the eldest skater at the 2007 Games was Joe McDonald

from the USA at 85 years old. McDonald won gold medals in the 500, 1500, and 3000-metre races. After the closing ceremonies, his rented van was stolen, with all of his bags inside. The thief was caught with the help of the Calgary Police Service HAWCS helicopter.

Margaret Elm • Margaret, mother of national speed skating team members Selina and Steven Elm, (Olympic silver medallist and former world record holder in the men's 3000-metre), competed in the 2007 Masters Games at the age of 54. Steven's former national teammate and Olympic Oval skate shop manager James Monson helped Margaret train for the competition and prepared her equipment for the races. She competed in the 500, 1000 and 1500-metre distances where she finished 14th, 13th and 13th respectively.

Roy Whitney • Roy had one of his most memorable moments at the Olympic Oval

when he set a new 5000-metre world record of 9.59.57 for men over 70 years old at the Olympic Oval Finale in March 2000. He was 72 years old at the time. At the 2007 World Masters International Speed Skating Games, at the age of 81, he established a new world record of 10.59.20 in the men's over-80 category in the same 5000-metre, a record that still stands today.

"I had no idea I had established a new record until I saw the report of world records of 'VERDENS "Topp-50" BESTE VETERANER, MENN, Klasseinndeling i henhold til internasjonale veteranregler, 1 Juli, 2009', forwarded to me by my record setting friend, Ron Johnston in 2010. My thanks to all at the Olympic Oval who make it possible for ordinary skaters like me to skate, and for arranging and conducting competitions, for all to compete and establish personal achievements."

– Roy D. Whitney

Financial Downturn

Financial downturn creates change. Will the Oval survive?

In early 2009, Mark Greenwald left the Oval after close to five years as the director. Greenwald's departure was the first in a series of shake-ups at the facility.

Much of the turmoil was a result of the economic downturn of the time. The same year, the Olympic Oval Women's High Performance Hockey Program was cut, the Olympic Oval High Performance Cycling Program ended, and the Oval X-Treme hockey team was dissolved.

The lack of funding also affected other legacy venues built for the 1988

Olympics, and left Calgary's future as a centre for high performance sports training in question. Canada's top athletes in speed skating, bobsled, luge, skeleton and skiing (among others) were on edge about the survival of their training facilities.

At the news conference announcing the cuts to the Oval's funding and operations, Canada's top speed skaters pleaded for emergency funding to save the facility. The national speed skating team was preparing for the 2010 Olympic Winter Games and not having a training facility would jeopardize their success, and the success of other Canadian athletes heading to Vancouver. Beyond that, the long term repercussions to Canadian

athletes and the sport of speed skating would be devastating.

The Oval fell into financial trouble in 2008 after the Olympic Endowment Fund (OEF), created for the 1988 Calgary Winter Olympic Games, took a $40-million financial hit due to the struggling stock market. The facility relied on interest from the fund for operations, and it had dwindled down to concerning levels. As the cuts to operations at the Oval came fast and furious, it was apparent to everyone that a new model had to be implemented to save the facility. The pleas of the speed skaters, the amateur sports community, Olympic Oval supporters, and the public users of the facility did not fall on deaf ears, and plans were set in motion to find a solution.

On November 9, 2010, The Honourable Gary Lunn, Minister of State (Sport), announced that a revised trust agreement was in place to ensure future funding for the struggling facility. The money would continue to come from the Olympic Endowment Fund, but under a new funding model that would provide a much-needed immediate influx of cash. This would ensure the Oval would continue to offer the best training facilities and maintain its world-class reputation.

The Government of Canada, Winsport Canada, Speed Skating Canada, the University of Calgary and the Olympic Oval worked together to come to a solution, revis-

"Our job is to adapt to any challenge that comes our way. But how do you adapt to not having ice?"

– Kristina Groves

ing the funding agreement to allow the Oval to draw an immediate lump sum payment to address critical infrastructure requirements. This draw would be replenished, with any interest made, as the fund recovered. The Oval, under the new terms, would also receive annual funds to facilitate coach and athlete development.

The new terms of the agreement guaranteed the Olympic Oval would continue to operate for the next 20 years, offering high performance programs, community events and public skating to local, national and international visitors.

Challenge Accepted

Fun Fact

Kam was the lead ice-maker for the short track speed skating and figure skating venue at the 2010 Vancouver Winter Olympics. A memorable moment from the short track 500-metre finals was when Canadian Charles Hamelin won the gold medal. His girlfriend, Marianne St. Gelais, bolted at full speed from her seat to the ice and Kam being a true gentleman helped her make the flying leap over a few railings so she would make it safely to rink side for the gold medal famous kiss.

As the funding crisis put the Oval's future in question a new director was chosen to face the challenge of moving the facility forward.

Kam Kiland started working at the Olympic Oval in 2002 as Operations Manager. Jacques Thibault hired him in January, and Kam was sent to the Salt Lake City Winter Olympic Games a mere month later. With this trip, he was given a first-hand, immediate introduction to the results of the Oval's culture of success as he witnessed Canadians skate to podium finishes at the Games.

What Kiland initially thought would be a brief stay in Calgary, turned into a decade-plus long career at the facility. He took immediately to the passion, the commitment, and the pursuit of excellence that was evident in the people and the place. He gained a clear understanding as the years went by that the Oval was different from other facilities around the world – that the staff and the people were the foundation of its success. After successfully leading the Oval operations team, he moved into the role of Director of Operations for the Faculty of Kinesiology where he remained until 2009.

Kiland was promoted to Olympic Oval Director during the financial crisis of 2009 that crippled the funding for the Oval, and put its future in jeopardy. At this critical time, Kam witnessed first-hand the extent of the passion people had for the building. Staff, speed skaters and partners like Speed Skating Canada, the U of C, and Winsport rallied behind the Oval to save the facility. Kiland gave special credit to Speed Skating Canada for their support and for putting the Oval programs into the spotlight when it was needed most.

As the Oval's future was back on track, Kam continued at the helm and tirelessly promoted the facility in the community and abroad. He oversaw the $9.7-million roof refurbishment, was an Oval ambassador providing support at the 2010 Vancouver Winter Olympics, spearheaded many mechanical and structural upgrades, and lobbied to have the Olympic Oval host the 2012 Samsung ISU World Cup Short Track competition, the first since 2003.

In the summer of 2013, Kiland ended his tenure at the Olympic Oval to return to his family home in Saskatchewan and enter the next phase of his career. Part of his legacy will be the work he did to bring the facility through tough times and ensure it continues to provide world class programs setting the standard of excellence in speed skating and high performance sport for years to come. He paved a way forward for those who continue to carry the torch long into the future.

Caring for the Legacy

1997 -2000
• In 1997 the Olympic Oval celebrated its tenth anniversary and the facility was starting to show its age. A decade of regular use by athletes, public and the university community meant the building was in need of upgrades. Over the next three seasons the Oval underwent a number of changes to both its internal workings and external appearance.

1997 -1998
• One lane of running track replaced with Mondo running surface.
• Sheet rubber installed in the public skating area.
• Redesign of the Oval lounge.
• Ongoing internal drainage project.
• Upgrades to the existing refrigeration plant.

1998 -1999
• Room 30 on activity level transformed from classroom into regeneration facility.
• Wheelchair accessible doors installed at north and south entrances.
• Wooden components of south rink boards replaced with aluminum framing.
• Existing ice plant evaporative condenser raised and enclosed and a second condenser added.
• Lighting system replaced with state-of-the-art system to save power.
• New Model 700 Zamboni arrives.
• More exercise bikes installed for athletes.

1999 -2000
• Renovation to the sound deck and plans started for technology room and video processing location.
• Rubber safety floor installed on east side of building for cycling training.
• New pulley system installed on hockey ice for more efficient movement of protective netting.
• New detailed hockey scoreboard installed.
• Timing system upgrades.

The operations team works hard to keep the Oval running smoothly, and upgrades are completed on a regular basis to keep the facility in top form.

The Oval enters the New Millennium

As the new millennium arrived, the Oval incorporated more and more technology into its day to day operations. Renovations were completed to improve the look of the facility and make it more user-friendly to both athlete user groups and the general public. In 2009, the largest capital project in the Oval's history began – a $9.7-million roof refurbishment, to fix leaking that had been occurring since the building's construction.

2000 -2001	• New glass doors installed on main level for security and aesthetics.
	• West wall alterations to give Oval a fresh appearance and better acoustics.
	• Tradition of Excellence Hall of Fame under construction.
	• Safety panels added to observation deck railings.
	• New photocopier, skate sharpening and rockering machine, start gate (cycling) and Alge timing boards acquired.
	• North rink is dedicated to the short track speed skating program, south rink is dedicated to hockey.
	• Addition of new athlete database to streamline athlete tracking and communication.
	• Renovations to the Regeneration Clinic started.
	• Version Two of long track safety mats installed.

2001 -2002	• Computerized rockering machine purchased.
	• Upgrade to rubber floor.
	• New fire doors.
	• New carpeting in athlete stretching area.
	• New Monark bikes.
	• Upgrades to all washrooms.
	• Safety panels to railing on main level.
	• Phase 1 of the Hall of Fame completed and phase 2 started.
	• Renovations to the regeneration clinic completed.
	• New Zamboni, fork lift, tables, walk behind scrubber, electronic massage tables, hydroculators and ice machine.

2002	• Hot and cold tubs, ice machine, and new massage table added to Regeneration Clinic.
	• New hydraulic table and massage chair for those with limited mobility also added.
	• New POS system planned to handle athlete fees.
2005	• Air duct system installed which helps to control airflow and building temperatures cut heating costs by 25%.
	• Installation of new Daktronics 30 × 11 ft. video display board.

2006 -2007	• New sound system installed.
	• New Wige timing system implemented.
2009	• Roof project starts.
2011 -2012	• $9.7-million refurbishment project to fix water leakage in roof is complete.
	• Permanent viewing deck installed in lounge/boardroom.
	• New entry system and gates installed at Guest Services for tracking user groups.
	• Weight room is updated with rubber floor.
	• New LED screens installed.

Women's Hockey Locker Room

It was clear after the first season of the Oval High Performance Women's Hockey Program that the bench style locker room could not accommodate the needs of the players. With the growth of the program, it quickly became evident to the coaches and program coordinator that the women needed a proper locker room. The few hooks provided above the benches were not sufficient to air out equipment properly between sessions.

In the summer of 1997, prior to new players arriving to join the program and the Summer Hockey Camp for Girls, program coordinator Leah Lacroix (Wood), men's Dinos hockey equipment manager Robin McDonald, and many of the current players rolled up their sleeves and proceeded to design, paint and build themselves a locker room and shooting gallery in north storage. The Oval maintenance team kicked in to provide the installation. Over the years, this locker room was upgraded to feature Oval X-Treme team colours, additional lockers and is presently painted U of C Dinos red and gold.

Oval X-Treme Dynasty

The Oval X-Treme was the elite amateur women's hockey team that trained as part of the Olympic Oval International High Performance Female Hockey Program between 1995 and 2009.

In 2009 the Calgary Oval X-Treme took a one-year leave of absence from the Western Women's Hockey League. The hiatus was a direct result of funding cuts that threatened not only the high performance women's hockey program, but the entire Olympic Oval facility.

Due to the financial crisis of 2009, the Oval X-Treme and the entire high performance female hockey program folded in June of 2009, along with the Olympic Oval's high performance cycling programs. Sacrifices were made in the building to preserve its core programs in long track and short track speed skating.

Oval X-Treme Championships

- NWHL Division titles won:
  2002-2003, 2003-2004

- Championship of the NWHL:
  2002-2003, 2003-2004

- WWHL Regular season titles won:
  2004-2005, 2005-2006, 2006-2007, 2007-2008, 2008-2009

- WWHL Champions cup: 2004-2005, 2005-2006, 2006-2007, 2007-2008

- Esso Canadian national championships won: 1998, 2001, 2003, 2007

The team filled a need for an elite women's team that could compete on the national stage. At the time, other cities in Canada were also developing teams at this level.

The X-Treme quickly formed a heated rivalry with their northern counterparts, the Edmonton Chimos. The first initiative that brought the two teams together was the Cameron Cup. This was a 16 game series between the X-Treme and the Chimos, with the winner representing Alberta at the Canadian Esso Nationals. The need for more competition was evident in order to take the players to another level.

In 2002 these two Alberta teams joined the newly formed National Women's Hockey League (NWHL), along with other Canadian teams, including the Vancouver Griffins, Brampton Thunder and Montreal Avalanche. After the 2003-2004 season, due to prohibitive costs to fly east, the western teams left the NWHL to form the five team Western Women's Hockey League (WWHL).

Over their history in the WWHL, the Oval X-Treme won three division titles, three regular season titles and six league championships. They were the undisputed powerhouse of women's hockey in western Canada, winning five consecutive league championships and compiling a regular season stat of 95-3-2-1 in their last five seasons. In addition to their success in the league they took home gold medals in the Esso Canadian National Championships in 1998, 2001, 2003 and 2007.

Because of the cross-over in training between the Oval X-Treme and the Canadian national women's hockey team, many of the players were involved in both. Typically, eight or nine of the national team skated with the X-Treme. Over the years, the team featured many top Canadian female hockey players, including Danielle Goyette, Hayley Wickenheiser, Cassie Campbell, Jennifer Botterill, Tessa Bonhomme, Carla Macleod, Colleen Sostorics, Gina Kingsbury, Gillian Ferrari and Kelly Bechard.

With Glowing Hearts

- Total distance: 18,000 km

- Number of torchbearers: 7,342

- Countries crossed: Greece, Canada

- Final torchbearer: Robyn Perry, 12 years old

Vancouver 2010 Torch Relay

- Total distance: 45,000 km

- Number of torchbearers: 12,000

- Countries crossed: Greece, Canada

- This Olympic Torch Relay was the longest national relay ever held for the Winter Games. The flame was lit in Olympia on October 22, 2009 and was in Canada from October 2009 until February 12, 2010. The Olympic Flame visited over 1000 communities.

- Nearly 200 celebrations hosted by communities in every province and territory, including a visit to Alert, Nunavut, the northernmost permanently inhabited community in the world.

- Approximately 90% of Canada's population was within a one-hour drive of experiencing the Olympic Flame.

Vancouver 2010 Torch Relay Arrives

On the 81st day of the torch relay to Vancouver, the flame returned to Calgary and the cauldron at Olympic Plaza was relit. The Olympic Flame, a symbol of hope for the future, a reflection of the past and Calgary hosting the 1988 Olympics was greeted with great enthusiasm by the community. Robyn Perry (now Ainsworth), who was 12 years old when she lit the flame in 1988, was chosen to light the flame once more. On the 82nd day, the torch was brought to the Olympic Oval.

Olympic Oval Wall of Champions inductees Susan Auch and (soon to be inducted) Kristina Groves ran the torch through the city with Frank King, Chairman and CEO of OCO '88. They brought it to the Oval on January 19, 2010, where Susan Auch handed it to Calgary Speed Skating Association skater Kyle Yoshida. Together with the Canadian national speed skating team they skated a lap of the Oval ice in front of a large crowd of supporters and fans. The excitement was palpable, with 25 days to go until the opening of the 2010 Vancouver Games.

"This place is the medal factory for Canada. Still. All these years later. At the next Olympics people will be asking: 'What is speed skating going to produce?' Well, what's produced is here."

– Marcel Lacroix

Bringing it Home

XXI Olympic Winter Games, Vancouver, Canada – February 12-28, 2010

In 2010 the Winter Olympic Games were held in Vancouver, and the excitement of seeing Canadian athletes compete on home soil was contagious as Canada celebrated the red and white from coast-to-coast-to-coast. Olympic Oval athletes played pivotal roles during the opening ceremonies for the Vancouver Games.

10 Once again the world watched the torch run into the Olympic Stadium. Man in Motion Rick Hanson, who was also in the Calgary '88 Opening Ceremonies, carried the torch into B.C. place and passed it to Olympic speed skating medallist and Olympic Oval Associate Director Catriona Le May Doan. It was subsequently handed to Canadian basketball great Steve Nash, and then to the Great One himself, hockey legend Wayne Gretzky. All four national sports icons, each carrying a torch, then walked to the cauldron to ignite the base, composed of what looked like giant shards of ice emerging from the stadium floor. Four "shards" were supposed to rise to greet the four torch bearers, but only three appeared, leaving Le May Doan without anything to light.

As the athletes marched in, the Canadian team was led by one of Canada's most decorated Olympians, Oval trained long track speed skater Clara Hughes. She was chosen as flag bearer for her achievements on the international stage, in both the Summer and Winter Olympics, as well as for her work as a humanitarian and activist. As flag bearer, she followed in the footsteps of other Oval alumni, including hockey phenom Danielle Goyette (Torino 2006) and fellow speed skater and Olympic medallist Catriona Le May Doan (2002). Oval trained Dinos Women's Hockey team captain Hayley Wickenheiser read the Athlete Oath.

Olympic Oval speed skaters were at the top of the podium often, showing their dominance in both short and long track events. Coached by long time Oval coach Marcel Lacroix, Denny Morrison, Lucas Makowsky, and Mathieu Giroux won the gold medal in the men's Team Pursuit and Christine Nesbitt also took home a gold medal, showing her unstoppable strength in the women's 1000-metre distance. Oval coach Xiuli Wang supported Kristina Groves to win two medals in what would be her last Olympic Games. She won a silver in the women's 1500-metre race and a bronze in

the 3000-metre event. Clara Hughes capped off her Olympic speed skating career with a bronze in the women's 5000-metre event. In the short track events, Jessica Gregg, coached by another Oval coach, Jonathon Cavar, was part of the women's 3000-metre relay team that won the silver medal.

Not only did Oval athletes and coaches win medals, but many skated in their first Games and achieved strong finishes. Brittany Schussler, Anastasia Bucsis, Kyle Parrott and Jamie Gregg all competed in long track events.

At home in Calgary, the Olympic Oval was a hub of activity and energy prior to and during the Games, with Oval trained athletes working hard to race toward best ever finishes in Vancouver. Those who were not able to make it to Vancouver in person gathered in the Olympic Oval lounge to watch Canadian athletes achieve their best performances ever at an Olympic Games.

Oval Trained Athletes in Vancouver

- **Speed Skating:** Anastasia Bucsis, Mathieu Giroux, Jamie Gregg, Kristina Groves, Clara Hughes, Mike Ireland, Cindy Klassen, Lucas Makowsky, Denny Morrison, Christine Nesbitt, Tamara Oudenaarden, Kyle Parrott, Shannon Rempel, Brittany Schussler, Jeremy Wotherspoon

- **Short Track:** Jessica Gregg

- **Women's Hockey:** Tessa Bonhomme, Gina Kingsbury, Carla MacLeod, Cherie Piper, Colleen Sostorics, Hayley Wickenheiser

Along with these Canadian Olympians many athletes, coaches and support staff called the Oval home prior to participating in these Olympics.

Clara Hughes

Olympic Oval Wall of Champions Inductee 2013

Clara shares the title of most decorated Canadian Olympian with fellow speed skater and teammate Cindy Klassen, each having accumulated a total of six Olympic medals over their illustrious careers. Hughes also has the distinction of being one of the few athletes who has medalled in both the Summer and Winter Olympics. She represented Canada in the sport of speed skating at the 2002, 2006 and 2010 Winter Games, and was on the Canadian Olympic cycling team at the 1996, 2000 and 2012 Summer Games.

Her impressive medal count includes: two bronze medals in cycling at the 1996 Summer Olympics in Atlanta, a bronze medal in the women's 5000-metre at the 2002 Winter Games in Salt Lake, a gold (women's 5000-metre) and silver (Team Pursuit) medal in 2006 in Turin, and a bronze medal again in the 5000-metre from Vancouver 2010.

Her career as a high performance athlete began in 1988, inspired after seeing Gaétan Boucher skate at the '88 Games in Calgary on the Olympic Oval that would eventually become her home ice. She switched from speed skating to cycling in 1990, and returned to speed skating, coached by Xiuli Wang, after the Summer Olympics in Sydney in 2000. The impetus for her return to speed skating was in part because of a tragic cycling accident in which her friend and teammate Nicole Reinhart was killed. Clara felt she needed to achieve all she could as an athlete while she was still healthy, had the ability, and was at the top of her game.

In addition to her many Olympic successes, Hughes also set a world record in the 10,000-metre in March of 2005 at the Olympic Oval in Calgary and was the flag bearer at the opening ceremonies at the Vancouver 2010 Olympics, proudly leading her team into B.C. Place.

Her achievements in sport have afforded her many opportunities to work in the community, championing issues that are close to her heart. She has donated thousands of dollars of her own money to charities, including organizations such as Right to Play and Take a Hike. She has been honoured many times for her contributions, including being named an Officer of the Order of Canada in 2007 and given a star on Canada's Walk of Fame 2010. In November of 2010 she was also inducted into Canada's Sports Hall of Fame.

She is currently the spokesperson for Bell's Let's Talk campaign (an initiative she started after coming out about her own mental health struggles) designed to bring awareness and conversation about mental illness to communities across Canada.

Clara will soon be inducted on to the Olympic Oval Wall of Champions, a distinction given to only seven other speed skaters before her.

Oval Reunion

Oval staff, alumni, officials, athletes, volunteers and friends were reunited in Vancouver for the 2010 Winter Olympic Games.

Zamboni®

Frank J. Zamboni, the inventor of the Zamboni® ice resurfacing machine, made it his life's mission to produce great ice.

Much like the ice-makers at the Olympic Oval, he wanted his machines to create an environment where the ice was never a factor in the performance of the athletes. The equipment bearing his name has set the standard for the industry and innovation in ice-making.

The Zamboni® ice-resurfacer made its Olympic debut at the 1960 Winter Olympic Games in Squaw Valley, California. A total of six machines were used at those Games, and the first ever resurfacer for the 400-metre oval track was introduced. This oversized machine was the forerunner to the one used today at the Calgary Olympic Oval.

At the Oval, these machines are a big part of what it takes to maintain the reputation of The Fastest Ice in the World™. Throughout the Oval's 25 year history, the humble ice resurfacing machine has assisted in the creation of many moments to remember.

The Olympic Oval owns three ice-resurfacers. One of these machines is one-and-a-half times larger than a standard size Zamboni® and there is only one other such machine in Canada.

The machines shave one to three millimetres off the ice to remove dirt that has drifted onto the ice and several resurfacings are conducted on the Oval ice over the course of a normal day.

Resurfacing the ice is an art, and it takes a skilled hand to make the perfect surface. Each machine and each driver have their own unique personalities, and the ice differs depending on the machine and who's behind the wheel.

Practical applications aside, the appearance of the machines on the ice fascinates spectators and it has achieved a special place in defining the Canadian identity. Outside of their ice resurfacing duties, the Olympic Oval machines have been used at the annual Christmas Skate as Santa's "sleigh" and have given rides to Olympic athletes, dignitaries, Oval guests and children who are part of charity initiatives like Make-a-Wish Foundation and the Calgary Children's Hospital. Rides have been auctioned off to raise money for charity and programs at the Oval.

Olympic Oval 911

At the 2010 Vancouver Winter Olympic Games, two of the ice resurfacing machines being used at the Richmond Oval encountered problems, which resulted in two difficult days at the speed skating venue, and delays in two races – one being the men's 500-metre final. To ensure the rest of the speed skating events went off without a glitch, an ice-resurfacer from the Olympic Oval in Calgary was loaded on to a flatbed truck and shipped across the Rockies.

The Calgary machine was recruited because it is oversized and designed specifically for the needs of resurfacing the large 400-metre long track ice and because of its capability to create perfect ice conditions.

We've Got it Covered

In 2010, change was underway at the Olympic Oval as the new operating agreement was signed and plans got started for the $9.7-million roof refurbishment. The new roof would eliminate leaks and inefficiencies, and ensure Canadian athletes could continue to train and compete at home.

In November of 2010 it was announced that the federal government had revised the trust arrangement that was put in place for operations when the facility was built. Instead of relying on interest payments from the Olympic Endowment Fund, the Olympic Oval would receive a $10-million withdrawal to address immediate infrastructure requirements, the roof being one of them. The leaking roof caused water to drip onto the ice, which was a safety hazard for skaters.

During the refurbishment, each of the triangular porcelain and enamel panels were removed and repaired, and the old membrane and insulation stripped and replaced. The structure was then reassembled and put back in place, with a new membrane and insulation underneath. The project was unique in that one hundred percent of the original roof was recycled or reused for the build.

The 2011-2012 season opened with the unveiling of the long awaited newly refurbished roof. To celebrate, an open house was hosted for the community in October. Visitors enjoyed skating, face painting, sport demonstrations from speed skaters and various interactive sport displays from many of the Oval's sport partners. Over 1,800 people attended the event and the Oval was proud to share the newly opened facility with the Calgary community.

In December of 2011, the Olympic Oval was designated as a city-wide historic resource, which formally acknowledged the property as a significant part of Calgary's history.

"This is a new beginning," said Oval director Kameron Kiland. "We are resetting the clock on the world's best speed skating facility. Canada's speed skaters have a guaranteed home for the next 20 years."

The University of Calgary

No other university in the world boasts an indoor speed skating oval in the heart of their campus.

In many ways the Olympic Oval at the University of Calgary serves as a constant reminder to the community that dreams can and do come true – with perseverance and hard work.

The Olympic Oval is an important part of the Faculty of Kinesiology, partnering in research and providing unique opportunities for students, alumni, faculty and staff. It's an international landmark that reminds each of us that we can be better, that we can achieve.

The Oval also provides a unique setting for many of the University's programs and events.

The Active Living Learn-to-Skate program takes place several times a year at the Oval. Thousands of young Calgarians have taken their first steps on the same ice that produced Olympic medallists and U of C graduates, including Alanna Kraus-Handley and Kristina Groves. Every summer hopeful young hockey players flood the Oval with dreams of being the next Hayley Wickenheiser, who called the Oval home as a member of Canada's national women's team, the Oval X-Treme and University of Calgary Dinos.

The University's graduating classes also assemble at the Oval, and don the graduation gowns that signify their achieve-ments. These memories of graduation day are likely one reason that the annual University of Calgary Alumni Skate is so popular.

And finally, a fusion of Dinos pride and the Oval's culture of success and achievement has created many champions over the years. On any given morning the Oval reverberates with the sound of the University of Calgary Dinos training hard in the weight room or sprinting on the track. From time to time the Dinos fearsome mascot Rex can be seen on The Fastest Ice in the World ™, reminding us all that, in Calgary at least, Dinos still rule the world.

Juniors

Junior speed skaters and their Oval coaches demonstrate the potential for future ongoing international successes.

Many young athletes have developed their skills through programs and competitions at the Olympic Oval, and have learned valuable life skills by being part of the supportive environment.

World Junior Championships are held once a year. Canada has hosted the Short Track Junior World Championships three times since its inception in 1994: Calgary (1995), Montreal (1999), and Sherbrooke (2009). Oval-trained Andrew Lahey took home the bronze for Canada in both the 1998 and 2000 events.

The first junior men's competition in long track speed skating was held in 1971. It started as a men's only competition, women were included in 1973 and the Team Pursuit event was added in 2002. The World Junior Speed Skating Championships have been held in Canada four times, including twice in Calgary (1991 and 1996).

Oval athlete Mark Knoll claimed the silver medal in consecutive years (1995 and 1996) and Justin Warsylewicz was named World Junior Champion in 2004. In women's competition in 2003, Shannon Rempel became the second Canadian female in history to become World Junior Champion, 30 years after her predecessor Sylvia Burka.

Kristina Groves

Olympic Oval Wall of Champions Inductee 2013

Kristina was directly inspired to pursue her dreams and goals in the sport of speed skating by watching the 1988 Winter Olympics on television as a young girl. The very construction of the Olympic Oval and seeing the facility shine during the '88 Games planted the seed that she too could reach the podium. Once she moved to Calgary to train it became the birthplace of her potential as a skater, and home to many of her dearest friends and supporters.

Groves relocated to Calgary from Ottawa. Her first serious competition was the 1996 Canadian All-Round Championships, and she started competing at world cups the same year. Her path to success as a speed skater began at the 1999 Canadian Championships, where she won gold in the 1500-metre and 3000-metre events, a silver in the 5000-metre, and finished second overall.

She competed in three winter Olympics during her career. She did not reach the podium at her first Games in Salt Lake City in 2002, but achieved double-medal performances at both the 2006 Winter Games in Turin and at the 2010 Vancouver Games at home.

Her two silver medals at 2006 Torino Winter Olympics (one in the 1500-metre and the other in the Team Pursuit), her first world cup wins in the 1500-metre distance in 2007, her five medals in five different distances (500, 1000, 1500, 3000 and 5000 metres) at the 2008 World Championships in Nagano, Japan, and her two Olympic medals in Vancouver (silver in the 1500-metre and bronze in the 3000-metre) are only some of the highlights of her long and successful career.

The Olympic Oval also provided Kristina with opportunities outside of speed skating. The facility's location on the U of C campus allowed her to pursue her Bachelor's Degree in Kinesiology while she was training. She also met her partner, Scott Maw, during her time at the Oval.

In 2011, Groves retired from competitive speed skating. She continues her involvement in sport as a colour commentator alongside Steve Armitage for CBC Sports. She also gives her support to charitable organizations Right to Play and Clean Air Champions, and was a founding member of Speed Skating Canada's sustainability committee. At the 2013 Essent ISU World Cup, Kristina Groves joined fellow long track Olympic Oval alumni Catriona Le May Doan, Susan Auch, Jeremy Wotherspoon, and Kevin Crockett as her banner was raised on to the Olympic Oval Wall of Champions.

Kristina Groves Career Highlights

- 2008 World Champion – 3000-metre
- 2-time World All-Round Championships, silver medallist
- 3-time Speed Skating Canada Female Athlete of the Year
- 4 Olympic medals
- Canada's most decorated World Single Distances Championships speed skater with 13 medals
- Canadian Spirit of Sport Award
- Graduate of the Last Decade, University of Calgary
- Olympic Oval Wall of Champions Inductee
- Queen Elizabeth II Diamond Jubilee Medal
- World Record, Team Pursuit (on Oval ice)

Wall of Champions

KRISTINA GROVES

JEREMY WOTHERSPOON

KEVIN CROCKETT

SUSAN AUCH

CATRIONA LE MAY DOAN

Alanna Kraus

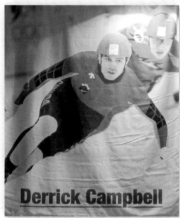

Derrick Campbell

The Olympic Oval Wall of Champions honours retired Canadian speed skaters who have made their mark on the international stage by winning individual or Team Pursuit/Relay Olympic medals.

To be inducted, these athletes need to have been training at the Oval when they won their medals and in good standing. The Oval tradition is to pay tribute to these outstanding athletes during international events such as world cup or World Championships. Over the past 25 years, a total of seven speed skaters have been presented with tribute banners and inducted on to the Olympic Oval Wall of Champions.

25th Anniversary Celebrations

Throughout the 2012-2013 season, the Olympic Oval celebrated its 25th anniversary and the 25th anniversary of the opening of the 1988 Winter Olympic Games in Calgary. Special events and world class competitions took place to mark the milestone.

The first special event of the year was the Olympic Oval London Lounge (pre-anniversary Olympic celebration). The Lounge opened for guests to view Canada's broadcast of the 2012 Summer Olympic Games from July 27-August 12, 2012. The event saw the main floor Oval lounge transformed into the Olympic Oval London Lounge, offering broadcast viewing of the Games, highlighting athletes who trained in the Oval's high performance weight room and on the track who were competing in London 2012. British consul-general Tony Kay was a surprise special guest to open the lounge, and poured the ceremonial first cup of tea.

The season truly kicked off with the annual Olympic Oval Gala presented by United Communities and Morrison Homes. On September 27, 2012, exactly 25 years to the day the Olympic Oval was officially opened in 1987, the black-tie evening was the inaugural event for the new Markin McPhail Centre at Winsport. Over $44,000 was raised for the Olympic Oval Athlete Bursary Fund and speed skating programs through raffles and silent and live auctions. Six athletes were awarded $1,000 bursaries each from funds raised at this event.

The Olympic Oval continued its tradition of holding world class competitions, with two world cup events held at the facility during the 2012-2013 season. For the first time in ten years the Olympic Oval was proud to host the Samsung ISU World Cup Short Track competition from October 19-21, 2012. This event brought the Oval, AASSA and SSC together as organizers to bring exciting short track action to the facility. The Intact Insurance School of Speed program was a tremendous success with over 960 school children attending and cheering on their favourite teams.

During the competition, U.S. short track national team skater J.R. Celski became the first athlete ever to break the seemingly impossible barrier of skating under 40 seconds in a 500-metre short track race. His time was an impressive 39.93. This was a significant accomplishment for the Olympic Oval and the ice crew. In total, six world records were broken during the exciting event.

The Short Track World Cup event also saw Alanna Kraus-Handley honoured for her athletic accomplishments, continuing the Oval's long-standing tradition of paying tribute to retired Olympic medallists that have called the Oval home.

Further on into the season, the Organizing Committee Calgary and SSC brought another prestigious competition to speed skating fans in Calgary. The Essent ISU World Cup Sprint Speed Skating took place January 19-20, 2013. Again the Oval ice proved to be The Fastest Ice in the World™ when female Korean skater Sang-Hwa Lee smashed the ladies 500-metre world record with a time of 36.80.

Continuing the tradition, the Olympic Oval was thrilled to recognize retired Olympic medallist Kristina Groves during the Essent ISU World Cup. Kristina started speed skating at the age of 11, after watching Canadian Gaétan Boucher compete at the Oval during the 1988 Calgary Winter Olympics. Twenty-five years later her banner was hoisted on to the Wall of Champions over the same ice that inspired her as a child.

To close out the season, the Olympic Oval Finale was the largest ever. Over 345 local, national, and international athletes skated in the competition. Again the ice conditions were fantastic and 872 personal bests were achieved and 16 national records were broken.

Cauldron Refurbishment

On January 23, 2013, The Olympic Oval welcomed back the refurbished Olympic Oval Cauldron for the 25th anniversary of the 1988 Calgary Winter Olympic Games. The refurbishment was a timely gift from ATCO Gas to mark the 25th anniversary of the Oval and its place as a legacy facility at the University of Calgary and for the city of Calgary. ATCO Gas completed the re-installation process of the cauldron at the north entrance of the Olympic Oval underneath The Spire. A crowd of Oval staff and athletes, University and ATCO Gas representatives, Calgarians, and local and national media gathered.

Celebrate '88 – Legacy Day

In addition to the world class competitions, the 25th anniversary season was topped off with special events to recognize the opening of the facility and anniversary of the 1988 Winter Olympic Games in Calgary. Two separate events were held on February 13 to mark the occasion. A daytime event, Celebrate '88 – Reignite the Spirit, saw Dr. Roger Jackson, Mayor Naheed Nenshi, University of Calgary President Dr. Elizabeth Cannon, four-time Olympic medallist Kristina Groves, Hidy & Howdy, and other special guests join the Olympic Oval and the University of Calgary as we shared the legacy and reignited the Olympic Cauldron.

Frank King, OCO '88 chairman (on behalf of City Council and Calgary Mayor Naheed Nenshi), read a special proclamation declaring February 13 "Olympic Legacy Day".

The festivities continued in the evening of February 13 with Celebrate 88 – Legacy Skate, a retro-skating party that featured DJ Rob Faust, Calgary 2012 artist-in-residence Ramin Eshraghi-Yazdi, Intact Insurance Pin Trading Zone and The RE/MAX athlete autograph sessions. This free public event drew over 1,000 people dressed in '80's retro outfits and official 1988 Winter Olympic Games clothing. The Calgary Sun and QR77 Radio were the media sponsors for the evening.

The Future Looks Bright

Olympic Oval speed skating camp participants, Oval program athletes and coaches set their sights high to carry the Oval legacy into the future.

Christine Nesbitt

Christine was an elite athlete at an early age. She started winning medals in speed skating at 13, and in 2003 she relocated from London, Ontario to Calgary to attend the University of Calgary as an engineering student. In 2005 she qualified for the Canadian national long track team.

Her biggest motivation came after the 2006 Torino Winter Games when together with her teammates she won a Team Pursuit silver medal. She was inspired by fellow athletes and teammates Cindy Klassen, Clara Hughes and Kristina Groves who returned home with multiple medals and Olympic glory. Nesbitt realized she had the same drive, desire and resources to achieve individual and international success. By the end of the 2008-2009 season, Christine's determination, drive and desire resulted in a massive windfall. She collected 10 bronze, 17 silver, and five gold medals at world cup events, and three gold, one silver, and two bronze medals at World Championship events. The four year road to Vancouver culminated in an unforgettable proud Canadian moment when she won a gold medal in the 1000-metre event at the Vancouver Olympics.

One of the biggest highlights of Christine Nesbitt's career came in Calgary at the 2012 World Sprint Championships on January 28, 2012 when she set the world record in the 1000-metre with a time of 1.13.11 on home-ice. Friends, fans and her Oval family looked on with excitement as she smashed the record set by Cindy Klassen six years earlier on the same ice.

As the Oval celebrates its 25th, Christine Nesbitt is celebrating her 10th year in the building. As she looks to the future and Sochi in 2014, she also looks back on her time with the understanding that she received everything she needed to perform at her highest level as an athlete. She seized these opportunities to make memories not only for herself, but for the nation.

Stats

"We didn't have a whole bunch of experience making speed skating ice at the beginning...but we proved them wrong."

– Mark Messer

Gathering Memories

Of all the records, awards and achievements, the greatest of these are the supportive friendships, the love and the Oval family that will continue the Legacy of Excellence from the past, in the present moment and into the future.

Olympic Oval World Records

The Olympic Oval has seen 258 long track and 30 short track world records set on The Fastest Ice in the World™ between September 1987 and March 2013. This is an outstanding achievement for any sporting venue and is a testament to the excellence of the venue and athletes who compete here.

ISU Speed Skating World Records
Long Track – Senior Men

Senior Men	Country	Distance	Time/Pts.	Date
Uwe-Jens Mey	GDR	500-metre	36.45	Feb. 14, 1988
Dan Jansen	USA	500-metre	36.41	Mar. 19, 1992
Dan Jansen	USA	500-metre	36.02	Mar. 20, 1993
Dan Jansen	USA	500-metre	35.76	Jan. 30, 1994
Hiroyasu Shimizu	JPN	500-metre	35.39	Mar. 2, 1996
Hiroyasu Shimizu	JPN	500-metre	35.36	Mar. 28, 1998
Hiroyasu Shimizu ❶	JPN	500-metre	34.82	Mar. 28, 1998
✦ Jeremy Wotherspoon	CAN	500-metre	34.76	Feb. 20, 1999
✦ Jeremy Wotherspoon	CAN	500-metre	34.63	Jan. 29, 2000

Senior Men	Country	Distance	Time/Pts.	Date
✦ Jeremy Wotherspoon	CAN	2x500-metre	68.31	Mar. 15, 2008

Senior Men	Country	Distance	Time/Pts.	Date
✦ Kevin Scott ❷	CAN	1000-metre	1.12.54	Dec. 17, 1993
Yasunori Miyabe	JPN	1000-metre	1.12.37	Mar. 26, 1994
✦ Sylvain Bouchard	CAN	1000-metre	1.12.27	Dec. 22, 1995
✦ Kevin Overland	CAN	1000-metre	1.12.19	Dec. 23, 1995
Manabu Horii	JPN	1000-metre	1.11.67	Mar. 1, 1996
Manabu Horii	JPN	1000-metre	1.10.63	Nov. 22, 1997
Jan Bos	NED	1000-metre	1.10.63	Nov. 22, 1997
Kyou-Hyuk Lee	KOR	1000-metre	1.10.42	Nov. 23, 1997
✦ Jeremy Wotherspoon	CAN	1000-metre	1.10.16	Dec. 29, 1997
✦ Sylvain Bouchard	CAN	1000-metre	1.09.60	Mar. 29, 1998
✦ Jeremy Wotherspoon	CAN	1000-metre	1.09.09	Jan. 15, 1999
✦ Jeremy Wotherspoon	CAN	1000-metre	1.08.66	Feb. 20, 1999
Jan Bos	NED	1000-metre	1.08.55	Feb. 21, 1999
✦ Jeremy Wotherspoon	CAN	1000-metre	1.08.49	Jan. 12, 2000
✦ Jeremy Wotherspoon	CAN	1000-metre	1.08.35	Mar. 18, 2000
✦ Mike Ireland	CAN	1000-metre	1.08.34	Mar. 3, 2001

Senior Men	Country	Distance	Time/Pts.	Date
Igor Zhelezovsky	URS	1500-metre	1.52.50	Dec. 5, 1987
Andre Hoffmann	GDR	1500-metre	1.52.06	Feb. 20, 1988
Hiroyuki Noake	JPN	1500-metre	1.50.61	Mar. 2, 1996
KC Boutiette	USA	1500-metre	1.50.09	Mar. 15, 1997
✦ Neal Marshall	CAN	1500-metre	1.50.05	Mar. 16, 1997
✦ Kevin Overland	CAN	1500-metre	1.49.07	Nov. 29, 1997
Ådne Søndrål	NOR	1500-metre	1.46.43	Mar. 28, 1998
Jakko Jan Leeuwangh	NED	1500-metre	1.45.56	Jan. 29, 2000
Kyou-Hyuk Lee	KOR	1500-metre	1.45.20	Mar. 15, 2001
Shani Davis	USA	1500-metre	1.42.68	Mar. 19, 2006
Shani Davis	USA	1500-metre	1.42.32	Mar. 4, 2007
✦ Denny Morrison	CAN	1500-metre	1.42.01	Mar. 14, 2008

Senior Men	Country	Distance	Time/Pts.	Date
Thomas Bos	NED	3000-metre	3.56.16	Apr. 3, 1992
Bob de Jong	NED	3000-metre	3.53.06	Mar. 8, 1996
Bart Veldkamp	BEL	3000-metre	3.48.91	Mar. 21, 1998
✦ Steven Elm	CAN	3000-metre	3.45.23	Mar. 19, 1999
✦ Steven Elm	CAN	3000-metre	3.43.76	Mar. 17, 2000
Gianni Romme	NED	3000-metre	3.42.75	Aug. 11, 2000
Chad Hedrick	USA	3000-metre	3.39.02	Mar. 10, 2005
Eskil Ervik	NOR	3000-metre	3.37.28	Nov. 5, 2005

Senior Men	Country	Distance	Time/Pts.	Date
Geir Karlstad ❸	NOR	5000-metre	6.43.59	Dec. 4, 1987
Gianni Romme	NED	5000-metre	6.21.49	Mar. 27, 1998
Gianni Romme	NED	5000-metre	6.18.72	Jan. 30, 2000
Chad Hedrick	USA	5000-metre	6.09.68	Nov. 13, 2005
Sven Kramer	NED	5000-metre	6.07.48	Mar. 3, 2007
Sven Kramer ❹	NED	5000-metre	6.03.32	Nov. 17, 2007

Senior Men	Country	Distance	Time/Pts.	Date
Geir Karlstad	NOR	10,000-metre	13.48.51	Dec. 6, 1987
Tomas Gustafson	SWE	10,000-metre	13.48.20	Feb. 21, 1988
Gianni Romme	NED	10,000-metre	13.08.71	Mar. 29, 1998
Sven Kramer	NED	10,000-metre	12.51.60	Mar. 19, 2006

Senior Men	Country	Distance	Time/Pts.	Date
Dan Jansen	USA	Sprint Comb.	145.58	Mar. 19-20, 1993
Dan Jansen	USA	Sprint Comb.	144.815	Jan. 29-30, 1994
Yasunori Miyabe	JPN	Sprint Comb.	144.445	Mar. 25-26, 1994
Manabu Horii	JPN	Sprint Comb.	143.425	Mar. 1-3, 1996
✦ Jeremy Wotherspoon	CAN	Sprint Comb.	141.995	Nov. 22-23, 1997
✦ Jeremy Wotherspoon	CAN	Sprint Comb.	140.05	Jan. 15-16, 1999
✦ Jeremy Wotherspoon	CAN	Sprint Comb.	138.31	Feb. 20-21, 1999
✦ Jeremy Wotherspoon	CAN	Sprint Comb.	137.23	Jan. 18-19, 2003
Stefan Groothuis	NED	Sprint Comb.	136.810	Jan. 28-29, 2012

Senior Men	Country	Distance	Time/Pts.	Date
Falko Zandstra	NED	Small Comb.	156.059	Mar. 1-3, 1991
KC Boutiette	USA	Small Comb.	154.103	Mar. 14-15, 1997
Carl Verheijen	NED	Small Comb.	153.767	Mar. 20-21, 1998
Erben Wennemars	NED	Small Comb.	153.583	Aug. 15-16, 1998
✦ Steven Elm	CAN	Small Comb.	152.043	Nov. 27-29, 1998
Christian Breuer	GER	Small Comb.	149.283	Mar. 19-20, 1999
Erben Wennemars	NED	Small Comb.	149.188	Aug. 14-15, 1999
Jochem Uytdehaage	NED	Small Comb.	147.665	Mar. 15-17, 2001
Erben Wennemars	NED	Small Comb.	146.355	Aug. 12-14, 2005

Senior Men	Country	Distance	Time/Pts.	Date
Roberto Sighel	ITA	Big Comb.	157.15	Mar. 21-22, 1992
Chad Hedrick	USA	Big Comb.	148.799	Jan. 21-22, 2006
Shani Davis	USA	Big Comb.	145.742	Mar. 18-19, 2006

Senior Men	Country	Distance	Time/Pts.	Date
✦ CANADA	CAN	Team Pursuit	3.39.69	Nov. 12, 2005

Most Memorable Moments:

❶ Hiroyasu Shimizu JPN 500-metre 34.82 Mar. 28, 1998
  • First men's 500-metre under 35 seconds

❷ Kevin Scott CAN 1000-metre 1.12.54 Dec. 17, 1993
  • First 1000-metre world record at Oval and Canadian

❸ Geir Karlstad NOR 5000-metre 6.43.59 Dec. 4, 1987

❹ Sven Kramer NED 5000-metre 6.03.32 Nov. 17, 2007
  • 5000-metre – 20 years, difference of 40 seconds

ISU Speed Skating World Records
Long Track – Junior Men

Junior Men	Country	Distance	Time/Pts.	Date
◆ Jeremy Wotherspoon	CAN	500-metre	36.67	Mar. 1, 1996
Kyou-Hyuk Lee	KOR	500-metre	36.59	Mar. 8, 1996
◆ Jeremy Wotherspoon	CAN	500-metre	36.58	Mar. 23, 1996
Jae-Bong Choi	KOR	500-metre	36.30	Nov. 27, 1998
Masaaki Kobayashi	JPN	500-metre	36.23	Mar. 18, 2000
Masaaki Kobayashi	JPN	500-metre	35.93	Mar. 19, 2000
Tadashi Obara	JPN	500-metre	35.24	Mar. 24, 2002

Junior Men	Country	Distance	Time/Pts.	Date
◆ Jeremy Wotherspoon	CAN	1000-metre	1.14.11	Mar. 17, 1995
◆ Jeremy Wotherspoon	CAN	1000-metre	1.13.55	Dec. 22, 1995
◆ Jeremy Wotherspoon	CAN	1000-metre	1.13.35	Dec. 23, 1995
◆ Jeremy Wotherspoon	CAN	1000-metre	1.13.28	Mar. 1, 1996
◆ Jeremy Wotherspoon	CAN	1000-metre	1.13.14	Mar. 23, 1996
Jae-Bong Choi	KOR	1000-metre	1.10.87	Feb. 20, 1999
Masaaki Kobayashi	JPN	1000-metre	1.10.83	Mar. 18, 2000
Beorn Nijenhuis ❂	NED	1000-metre	1.10.65	Mar. 23, 2002
Beorn Nijenhuis ❂	NED	1000-metre	1.08.53	Jan. 19, 2003

Junior Men	Country	Distance	Time/Pts.	Date
Falko Zandstra	NED	1500-metre	1.53.26	Mar. 2, 1991
Yusuke Imai	JPN	1500-metre	1.52.88	Mar. 2, 1996
Yusuke Imai	JPN	1500-metre	1.52.78	Mar. 9, 1996
Yusuke Imai	JPN	1500-metre	1.52.33	Feb. 23, 1997
Dmitry Shepel	RUS	1500-metre	1.50.45	Mar. 21, 1998
Jae-Bong Choi	KOR	1500-metre	1.49.71	Nov. 28, 1998
Mark Tuitert	NED	1500-metre	1.48.45	Mar. 19, 1999
Shingo Doi	JPN	1500-metre	1.47.33	Mar. 17, 2001
Beorn Nijenhuis	NED	1500-metre	1.46.80	Mar. 22, 2002
Remco olde Heuvel	NED	1500-metre	1.46.73	Mar. 21, 2003
Sjoerd de Vries	NED	1500-metre	1.45.54	Mar. 15, 2007
Brian Hansen	USA	1500-metre	1.44.52	Dec. 5, 2009

Junior Men	Country	Distance	Time/Pts.	Date
Falko Zandstra	NED	3000-metre	3.57.64	Mar. 1, 1991
Bob de Jong	NED	3000-metre	3.53.06	Mar. 8, 1996
Mark Tuitert	NED	3000-metre	3.48.56	Mar. 19, 1999
Tom Prinsen	NED	3000-metre	3.46.75	Mar. 21, 2002
Remco olde Heuvel	NED	3000-metre	3.45.87	Mar. 20, 2003
Wouter olde Heuvel	NED	3000-metre	3.44.72	Mar. 10, 2005
Håvard Bøkko	NOR	3000-metre	3.43.66	Nov. 5, 2005
Håvard Bøkko	NOR	3000-metre	3.43.20	Mar. 21, 2006
Sjoerd de Vries	NED	3000-metre	3.42.98	Mar. 13, 2007

Junior Men	Country	Distance	Time/Pts.	Date
Yong-Hun Song	PRK	5000-metre	7.01.56	Feb. 17, 1988
Falko Zandstra	NED	5000-metre	6.47.10	Mar. 3, 1991
Bob de Jong	NED	5000-metre	6.37.55	Mar. 10, 1996
Mark Tuitert	NED	5000-metre	6.33.26	Mar. 20, 1999
Johan Röjler	SWE	5000-metre	6.32.92	Mar. 2, 2001
Hiroki Hirako	JPN	5000-metre	6.31.46	Mar. 2, 2001
Johan Röjler	SWE	5000-metre	6.31.10	Mar. 17, 2001
Tom Prinsen	NED	5000-metre	6.29.69	Mar. 21, 2002
Sven Kramer	NED	5000-metre	6.28.45	Mar. 12, 2004
Håvard Bøkko	NOR	5000-metre	6.18.93	Nov. 13, 2005

Junior Men	Country	Distance	Time/Pts.	Date
◆ Jeremy Wotherspoon	CAN	Sprint Comb.	148.350	Mar. 17-18, 1995
◆ Jeremy Wotherspoon	CAN	Sprint Comb.	147.300	Dec. 22-23, 1995
◆ Jeremy Wotherspoon	CAN	Sprint Comb.	146.465	Mar. 23-24, 1996
Jae-Bong Choi	KOR	Sprint Comb.	143.965	Feb. 20-21, 1999
Masaaki Kobayashi	JPN	Sprint Comb.	143.015	Mar. 19-20, 2000
Tadashi Obara	JPN	Sprint Comb.	141.985	Mar. 23-24, 2000
Beorn Nijenhuis	NED	Sprint Comb.	139.750	Jan. 18-19, 2003

Junior Men	Country	Distance	Time/Pts.	Date
Falko Zandstra	NED	Small Comb.	156.059	Mar. 1-3, 1991
Jae-Bong Choi	KOR	Small Comb.	153.689	Nov. 27-29, 1998
◆ Philippe Marois	CAN	Small Comb.	153.363	Mar. 17-18, 2000
Shingo Doi	JPN	Small Comb.	151.258	Mar. 15-17, 2001
Remco olde Heuvel	NED	Small Comb.	150.454	Mar. 20-22, 2002
Remco olde Heuvel	NED	Small Comb.	149.481	Mar. 19-21, 2003
Wouter olde Heuvel	NED	Small Comb.	148.614	Mar. 9-11, 2005
Berden de Vries	NED	Small Comb.	148.070	Mar. 12-14, 2008

Junior Men	Country	Distance	Time/Pts.	Date
Shingo Hashibami	JPN	Team Pursuit	3.59.31	Aug. 14, 2005
Toshiyuki Sayama				
Takumi Yui				
Zdenek Haselberger	CZE	Team Pursuit	3.55.26	Nov. 18, 2007
Pavel Kulma				
Milan Sáblik				

Most Memorable Moments:

❂ Beorn Nijenhuis NED 1000-metre 1.10.65 Mar. 23, 2002
  Beorn Nijenhuis NED 1000-metre 1.08.53 Jan. 19, 2003
  • Destroys his own world record

Olympic Oval World Records

ISU Speed Skating World Records
Long Track – Senior Women

Senior Women	Country	Distance	Time/Pts.	Date
Christa Rothenburger	GDR	500-metre	39.39	Dec. 6, 1987
Bonnie Blair	USA	500-metre	39.10	Feb. 22, 1988
Bonnie Blair	USA	500-metre	38.99	Mar. 26, 1994
Bonnie Blair	USA	500-metre	38.69	Feb. 12, 1995
✦ Catriona Le May Doan ❶	CAN	500-metre	37.90	Nov. 22, 1997
✦ Catriona Le May Doan	CAN	500-metre	37.90	Nov. 23, 1997
✦ Catriona Le May Doan	CAN	500-metre	37.71	Dec. 28, 1997
✦ Catriona Le May Doan	CAN	500-metre	37.55	Dec. 29, 1997
✦ Catriona Le May Doan	CAN	500-metre	37.40	Jan. 6, 2001
✦ Catriona Le May Doan	CAN	500-metre	37.29	Dec. 8, 2001
✦ Catriona Le May Doan	CAN	500-metre	37.22	Dec. 9, 2001
Jenny Wolf	GER	500-metre	37.02	Nov. 16, 2007
Jing Yu ❷	CHN	500-metre	36.94	Jan. 29, 2012
Sang-Hwa Lee ❸	KOR	500-metre	36.80	Jan. 19, 2013

Senior Women	Country	Distance	Time/Pts.	Date
Karin Kania	GDR	1000-metre	1.18.11	Dec. 5, 1987
Christa Rothenburger	GDR	1000-metre	1.17.65	Feb. 26, 1988
✦ Catriona Le May Doan	CAN	1000-metre	1.16.07	Nov. 22, 1997
Chris Witty	USA	1000-metre	1.15.43	Nov. 23, 1997
Chris Witty	USA	1000-metre	1.14.96	Mar. 28, 1998
Monique Garbrecht	GER	1000-metre	1.14.61	Feb. 21, 1999
Chris Witty	USA	1000-metre	1.14.58	Mar. 3, 2001
✦ Cindy Klassen	CAN	1000-metre	1.13.46	Mar. 24, 2006
✦ Cindy Klassen	CAN	1000-metre	1.13.11	Mar. 25, 2006
✦ Christine Nesbitt ❹	CAN	1000-metre	1.12.68	Jan. 28, 2012

Senior Women	Country	Distance	Time/Pts.	Date
✦ Catriona Le May Doan	CAN	1500-metre	1.57.87	Nov. 29, 1997
Anni Friesinger	GER	1500-metre	1.56.95	Mar. 29, 1998
Annamarie Thomas	NED	1500-metre	1.55.50	Mar. 20, 1999
Anni Friesinger	GER	1500-metre	1.54.38	Mar. 4, 2001
✦ Cindy Klassen	CAN	1500-metre	1.53.77	Oct. 28, 2005
Anni Friesinger	GER	1500-metre	1.53.22	Nov. 6, 2005

Senior Women	Country	Distance	Time/Pts.	Date
Gabi Zange	GDR	3000-metre	4.16.76	Dec. 5, 1987
Yvonne van Gennip	NED	3000-metre	4.11.94	Feb. 23, 1988
Gunda Kleemann	GER	3000-metre	4.10.80	Dec. 9, 1990
Gunda Niemann	GER	3000-metre	4.09.32	Mar. 25, 1994
Gunda Niemann-Stirnemann	GER	3000-metre	4.01.67	Mar. 27, 1998
Gunda Niemann-Stirnemann	GER	3000-metre	4.00.51	Jan. 30, 2000
Claudia Pechstein	GER	3000-metre	3.59.26	Mar. 2, 2001
✦ Cindy Klassen	CAN	3000-metre	3.55.75	Nov. 12, 2005
✦ Cindy Klassen	CAN	3000-metre	3.53.34	Mar. 18, 2006

Senior Women	Country	Distance	Time/Pts.	Date
Yvonne van Gennip	NED	5000-metre	7.14.13	Feb. 28, 1988
Gunda Niemann	GER	5000-metre	7.03.26	Mar. 26, 1994
Gunda Niemann-Stirnemann	GER	5000-metre	6.58.63	Mar. 28, 1998

Senior Women	Country	Distance	Time/Pts.	Date
Bonnie Blair	USA	Sprint Comb.	157.405	Jan. 29-30, 1994
Bonnie Blair	USA	Sprint Comb.	156.505	Mar. 25-26, 1994
Bonnie Blair	USA	Sprint Comb.	156.435	Feb. 11-12, 1995
✦ Catriona Le May Doan	CAN	Sprint Comb.	151.690	Nov. 22-23, 1997
Monique Garbrecht	GER	Sprint Comb.	151.605	Feb. 20-21, 1999
✦ Catriona Le May Doan	CAN	Sprint Comb.	150.085	Jan. 6-7, 2001
✦ Cindy Klassen	CAN	Sprint Comb.	149.305	Mar. 24-25, 2006
Jing Yu	CHN	Sprint Comb.	148.610	Jan. 28-29, 2012
Heather Richardson	USA	Sprint Comb.	147.735	Jan. 20, 2013

Senior Women	Country	Distance	Time/Pts.	Date
Emese Hunyady	AUT	Mini Comb.	164.658	Mar. 26-27, 1994
Annamarie Thomas	NED	Mini Comb.	163.901	Mar. 22-23, 1996
Marianne Timmer	NED	Mini Comb.	163.315	Mar. 15-16, 1997
Maki Tabata	JPN	Mini Comb.	162.731	Aug. 15-16, 1998
Becky Sundstrom	USA	Mini Comb.	161.439	Nov. 27-29, 1998
Annamarie Thomas	NED	Mini Comb.	158.183	Mar. 20-21, 1999
✦ Cindy Klassen	CAN	Mini Comb.	155.576	Mar. 15-17, 2001

Senior Women	Country	Distance	Time/Pts.	Date
✦ Cindy Klassen	CAN	Small Comb.	157.177	Jan. 21-22, 2006
✦ Cindy Klassen	CAN	Small Comb.	154.580	Mar. 18-19, 2006

Senior Women	Country	Distance	Time/Pts.	Date
Daniela Anschütz	GER	Team Pursuit	2.56.04	Nov. 13, 2005
Anni Friesinger				
Claudia Pechstein				
✦ Kristina Groves	CAN	Team Pursuit	2.55.79	Dec. 6, 2009
✦ Christine Nesbitt				
✦ Brittany Schussler				

Most Memorable Moments:

❶ Catriona Le May Doan CAN 500-metre
  • Breaks her own Olympic Oval World Record seven times in succession

❷ Jing Yu CHN 500-metre 36.94 Jan. 29, 2012
  • First women's 500-metre under 37 seconds

❸ Sang-Hwa Lee KOR 500-metre 36.80 Jan. 19, 2013
  • Most recent women's 500-metre

❹ Christine Nesbitt CAN 1000-metre 1.12.68 Jan. 28, 2012
  • Christine's Most Memorable Moment

ISU Speed Skating World Records
Long Track – Junior Women

Junior Women	Country	Distance	Time/Pts.	Date
Tomomi Shimizu	JPN	500-metre	39.85	Jan. 3, 1997
Seung-Yong Choi	KOR	500-metre	39.72	Nov. 28, 1998
Seung-Yong Choi	KOR	500-metre	39.55	Nov. 29, 1998
Sayuri Osuga	JPN	500-metre	38.58	Jan. 29, 2000
✤ Shannon Rempel	CAN	500-metre	38.53	Mar. 22, 2003
Sayuri Yoshii	JPN	500-metre	38.09	Mar. 13, 2004

Junior Women	Country	Distance	Time/Pts.	Date
Chris Witty	USA	1000-metre	1.20.77	Mar. 25, 1994
Anni Friesinger	GER	1000-metre	1.20.61	Mar. 9, 1996
Aki Tonoike	JPN	1000-metre	1.18.40	Nov. 22, 1997
Aki Tonoike	JPN	1000-metre	1.18.28	Nov. 23, 1997
Sayuri Osuga	JPN	1000-metre	1.17.49	Jan. 30, 2000
Sayuri Osuga	JPN	1000-metre	1.17.33	Mar. 18, 2000
Heike Hartmann	GER	1000-metre	1.16.92	Mar. 3, 2001
Judith Hesse	GER	1000-metre	1.16.14	Mar. 22, 2002
Ireen Wüst ◉	NED	1000-metre	1.15.93	Mar. 11, 2005
Laurine van Riessen	NED	1000-metre	1.15.53	Mar. 16, 2007
Marrit Leenstra	NED	1000-metre	1.15.41	Mar. 13, 2008

Junior Women	Country	Distance	Time/Pts.	Date
Svetlana Bazhanova	URS	1500-metre	2.05.14	Mar. 2, 1991
Becky Sundstrom	USA	1500-metre	2.05.00	Mar. 18, 1995
Anni Friesinger	GER	1500-metre	2.03.72	Mar. 1, 1996
Kirstin Holum	USA	1500-metre	2.03.61	Mar. 22, 1997
Kirstin Holum	USA	1500-metre	2.01.87	Jan. 24, 1998
Aki Tonoike	JPN	1500-metre	2.01.79	Mar. 29, 1998
Catherine Raney	USA	1500-metre	2.00.37	Mar. 20, 1999
Song Li	CHN	1500-metre	2.00.04	Jan. 29, 2000
Elma de Vries	NED	1500-metre	1.58.93	Mar. 21, 2002
Ireen Wüst	NED	1500-metre	1.58.10	Mar. 11, 2004
Ireen Wüst	NED	1500-metre	1.56.69	Mar. 10, 2005
Marrit Leenstra	NED	1500-metre	1.55.14	Mar. 12, 2008

Junior Women	Country	Distance	Time/Pts.	Date
Svetlana Bazhanova	URS	3000-metre	4.21.59	Mar. 2, 1991
Nami Nemoto	JPN	3000-metre	4.18.88	Mar. 25, 1994
Anni Friesinger	GER	3000-metre	4.17.04	Mar. 3, 1996
Catherine Raney	USA	3000-metre	4.11.83	Mar. 27, 1998
Song Li	CHN	3000-metre	4.10.30	Jan. 30, 2000
Elma de Vries	NED	3000-metre	4.09.66	Mar. 22, 2002
Ireen Wüst	NED	3000-metre	4.08.64	Mar. 12, 2004
Ireen Wüst	NED	3000-metre	4.07.71	Mar. 10, 2005
Martina Sáblíková	CZE	3000-metre	4.03.35	Nov. 12, 2005
Martina Sáblíková	CZE	3000-metre	4.00.63	Mar. 22, 2006

Junior Women	Country	Distance	Time/Pts.	Date
Chris Witty	USA	Sprint Comb.	162.820	Mar. 25-26, 1994
Tomomi Shimizu	JPN	Sprint Comb.	161.050	Jan. 3-4, 1997
Seung-Yong Choi	KOR	Sprint Comb.	158.785	Nov. 28-29, 1998
Sayuri Osuga	JPN	Sprint Comb.	155.565	Mar. 18-19, 2000
✤ Shannon Rempel	CAN	Sprint Comb.	154.725	Jan. 2-3, 2003
✤ Shannon Rempel	CAN	Sprint Comb.	154.480	Jan. 18-19, 2003
Karolina Erbanová	CZE	Sprint Comb.	152.470	Jan. 28-29, 2012

Junior Women	Country	Distance	Time/Pts.	Date
Anke Baier	GER	Mini-Comb.	169.124	Mar. 1-3, 1991
Becky Sundstrom	USA	Mini-Comb.	167.819	Mar. 18-19, 1995
Anni Friesinger	GER	Mini-Comb.	166.476	Mar. 8-10, 1996
Wieteke Cramer	NED	Mini-Comb.	162.452	Mar. 17-18, 2000
Elma de Vries	NED	Mini-Comb.	159.938	Mar. 20-22, 2002
Ireen Wüst	NED	Mini-Comb.	158.916	Mar. 11-12, 2004
Ireen Wüst	NED	Mini-Comb.	157.436	Mar. 9-11, 2005
Marrit Leenstra	NED	Mini-Comb.	156.360	Mar. 12-13, 2008

Most Memorable Moment:

◉ Ireen Wüst NED
• Breaks eight junior world records, seven set in Calgary

Olympic Oval World Records

ISU Speed Skating World Records
Short Track – Senior Men

Senior Men	Country	Distance	Time/Pts.	Date
✦ Jeffrey Scholten	CAN	500-metre	41.742	Mar. 4, 2000
✦ Jeffrey Scholten	CAN	500-metre	41.514	Oct. 13, 2001
✦ Jeffrey Scholten	CAN	500-metre	41.289	Mar. 8, 2003
✦ Jean-François Monette	CAN	500-metre	41.184	Oct. 18, 2003
✦ François Hamelin	CAN	500-metre	41.066	Oct. 13, 2007
Vladimir Grigorev	RUS	500-metre	40.458	Oct. 19, 2012
J.R. Celski Ⓜ	USA	500-metre	39.937	Oct. 21, 2012

Senior Men	Country	Distance	Time/Pts.	Date
✦ Jeffrey Scholten	CAN	1000-metre	1.26.970	Mar. 5, 2000
✦ Steve Robillard	CAN	1000-metre	1.25.985	Oct. 14, 2001
✦ Jean-François Monette	CAN	1000-metre	1.25.662	Mar. 9, 2003
✦ Michael Gilday	CAN	1000-metre	1.23.815	Oct. 14, 2007
Yoon-Gy Kwak	KOR	1000-metre	1:23.007	Oct. 21, 2012

Senior Men	Country	Distance	Time/Pts.	Date
✦ Andrew Quinn	CAN	1500-metre	2.15.495	Mar. 4, 2000
✦ Steve Robillard	CAN	1500-metre	2.15.383	Oct. 12, 2001
✦ Steve Robillard	CAN	1500-metre	2.12.234	Oct. 11, 2002

Senior Men	Country	Distance	Time/Pts.	Date
✦ Steve Robillard	CAN	3000-metre	4.38.061	Oct. 13, 2002

Most Memorable Moment:

Ⓜ J.R. Celski USA 500-metre 39.937 Oct. 21, 2012
 • First men's 500-metre under 40 seconds.

Senior Men	Country	Distance	Time/Pts.	Date
✦ Marc Gagnon	CAN	5000-metre relay	6.43.730	Oct. 14, 2001
✦ Jean-François Monette				
✦ Eric Bédard				
✦ Mathieu Turcotte				
✦ Jonathan Guilmette	CAN	5000-metre relay	6.43.667	Oct. 17, 2003
✦ Jeffrey Scholten				
✦ Eric Bédard				
✦ Mathieu Turcotte				
Suk-Woo Song	KOR	5000-metre relay	6.42.893	Oct. 18, 2003
Hyun-Soo Ahn				
Seung-Jae Lee				
Nam-Kyu Cho				
✦ Michael Gilday	CAN	5000-metre relay	6:30.958	Oct. 19, 2012
✦ Charles Hamelin				
✦ François Hamelin				
✦ Olivier Jean				

ISU Speed Skating World Records
Short Track – Junior Men

Junior Men	Country	Distance	Time/Pts.	Date
Seung-Chan Lee	KOR	1500-metre	2.25.53	Jan. 28, 1995

ISU Speed Skating World Records
Short Track – Senior Women

Senior Women	Country	Distance	Time/Pts.	Date
Evgenia Radanova	BUL	500-metre	43.671	Oct. 19, 2001

Senior Women	Country	Distance	Time/Pts.	Date
Yang Yang (A)	CHN	1000-metre	1.31.871	Oct. 20, 2001
Yang Yang (A)	CHN	1000-metre	1.31.191	Feb. 3, 2002
✦ Valerie Maltais	CAN	1000-metre	1.27.653	Oct. 19, 2012
Suk Hee Shim	KOR	1000-metre	1:26.661	Oct. 21, 2012

Senior Women	Country	Distance	Time/Pts.	Date
Yang Yang (A)	CHN	5000-metre relay	4.13.541	Oct. 19, 2001
Yang Yang (S)				
Cunlu Wang				
Dandan Sun				
Wei Wang	CHN	5000-metre relay	4.11.802	Oct. 18, 2003
Tianyu Fu				
Meng Wang				
Xiaolei Cheng				
Eun-Kyung Choi	CHN	5000-metre relay	4.11.742	Oct. 19, 2003
Min-Jee Kim				
Chun-Sa Byun				
Gi-Hyun Ko				

ISU Speed Skating World Records
Short Track – Junior Women

Junior Women	Country	Distance	Time/Pts.	Date
Yun-Mi Kim	KOR	500-metre	46.23	Jan. 28, 1995

Olympic Medals

The Olympic Oval is known as Canada's Medal Factory and Oval-trained athletes have won numerous medals at the Summer and Winter Olympics since the 1988 Calgary Games. Leading into the 2014 Sochi Olympics, Oval speed skaters have collected a total of 28 Winter Olympic medals.

Race	Olympic Games	Medal Count
Short Track Speed Skating Men's Relay	Albertville	●
Susan Auch, long track speedskating	Lillehammer	●
Catriona Le May Doan, long track speed skating	Nagano	● ●
Short Track Speed Skating Men's Relay	Nagano	●
Susan Auch, long track speed skating	Nagano	●
Jeremy Wotherspoon, long track speed skating	Nagano	●
Kevin Overland, long track speed skating	Nagano	●
Short Track Speed Skating Women's Relay	Nagano	●
Catriona Le May Doan, long track speed skating	Salt Lake City	●
Cindy Klassen, long track speed skating	Salt Lake City	●
Clara Hughes, long track speed skating	Salt Lake City	●
Short Track Speed Skating Women's Relay	Salt Lake City	●
Cindy Klassen, long track speed skating	Torino	● ● ● ●
Clara Hughes, long track speed skating	Torino	●
Kristina Groves, long track speed skating	Torino	●
Long Track Speed Skating Women's Pursuit	Torino	●
Long Track Speed Skating Men's Pursuit	Torino	●
Short Track Speed Skating Women's Relay	Torino	●
Christine Nesbitt, long track speed skating	Vancouver	●
Long Track Speed Skating Men's Pursuit	Vancouver	●
Kristina Groves, long track speed skating	Vancouver	● ●
Clara Hughes, long track speed skating	Vancouver	●
Short Track Speed Skating Women's Relay	Vancouver	●
TOTAL MEDAL COUNT		**28 MEDALS**

Credits

Director:
Kameron Kiland

Editorial Manager:
Leah Lacroix

Writer:
Tracy Stewart

Photo Editor:
Gillian Richmond

Official Photographer:
Arno Hoogveld

Research:
Leah Lacroix
Gillian Richmond
Tracy Stewart

Photo Research:
David Vink

Assistant Editors:
Kristina Groves
Shawn Holman
Darlene Kastner
Mark Messer

Stats:
Peter Dankers
John McClennan
Magne Teigen
Johan van
 den Heuvel
Georg Wiig

Design:
Ian Regier

Contributors

Thank you to all those who helped make the Olympic Oval's 25th anniversary book a reality. Your stories and memories are at the heart of what the Oval is about—the people. Over the years, the people who make up the Oval family have reached great heights and inspired others to follow their dreams. We appreciate the contributions of those who have been a part of the Oval's success, and we look forward to the next 25 years.

Joshua Ajohn
Alberta Amateur
 Speed Skating
 Association
Alberta Sports
 Hall of Fame
Alberta Volleyball
Adam Ashdown
ATCO Gas
Susan Auch
Brian Bahr
Greg Baker
Andrew Barron
Hall Beaulieu
Kelly Bechard
Robyn Beck
Zack Bell
Al Bello
John Berezuk
Kathy Berg
Sarah Bergeron
Stephanie Bergeron
Christopher Berry
Jo-Ann Billingsley
Bonnie Blair
 (Cruikshank)
Kristian Bogner
Thomas Borden
Brigitta Botyanszki
Jeff Bough
Michael Boyles
Riley Brandt
Benard Brault

Dave Brown
Dawn Brown
Douglas Brown
Laura Brown
Aaron Bruce
Built for Speed
 Documentary
Carolyn Burke
Stephen Burke
Cara Button
Calgary 2012
Calgary Booster Club
Calgary Herald
Calgary Inter-Faith
 Food Bank Society
Calgary Photo
 Scanning
Calgary Police
 Service
Calgary Speed
 Skating
 Association
Calgary Sun
Derrick Campbell
Cassie
 Campbell-Pascall
Canada Games
 Council
Canada's Sports
 Hall of Fame
Canadian Olympic
 Committee
Canadian Sport
 Institute Calgary
Jonathon Cavar

Goh Chai Hin
Paul Chaisson
Len Chan
City of Calgary
City of Calgary, City
 Clerks Office
City of Lethbridge
CJSW
Coaches of Canada
Bridget Cox
Kevin Crockett
Jeff Cruz
Luisa Currie
Telma Cuellar
Peter Dankers
Mark Dauwerse
Cory Davidson
Gloria Davis
Aletta de Rooij
Yvon DeBlois
Mechteld (Maggie)
 Dekking
Karen Delaney
Tara Doherty
 (Murray)
Craig Drevit
Stewart Dryden
Tanya Dubnicoff
Robert Dubreuil
Darryl Dyck
Chris Edwards
emc2 Events
Ramin Eshraghi-Yazdi

Tim Farstad
Fast Forward Weekly
Eric Feferberg
Elise and Pascal
 Ferraro
Frank Fife
Casey FitzRandolph
Jennifer
 FitzRandolph
Debbie Fisher
Flagworks
Andre Forget
Frank J. Zamboni
 Co., Inc.
Frank Fife
Deanne Frere
Kevin Frost
Annie Gagnon
Terry Gagnon
Pablo Galvez
David Garrison
Bev Garrow
Gault Museum
 Archives
Getty Images
Susie Gibbon (Bruce)
Duff Gibson
Brad Giesbrecht
Glen Co Photography
Glenbow Museum
GOFOTO
Darren Goldstein
Henrietta Goplen

Government of
 Alberta
Government of
 Canada
Danielle Goyette
Scott Grant
Mark Greenwald
Jessica Gregg
Sarah Gregg
Kristina Groves
Jonathan Guilmette
John Hales
Yves Hamelin
Kristy (Elisha)
 Hawrys
Dale Henwood
Ellie Hildebrandt
Tracy Hillis
Nannette
 Ho-Covernton
Dave Holland
Shawn Holman
Shirley Hons
Arno Hoogveld
Clara Hughes
Alice Humeny
Alexandra Ianculescu
Jaekyun Im
Sama Imamvredi
Impact Magazine
Kurt Innes
International
 Skating Union
Mike Ireland
Sean Ireland
Dr. Roger Jackson
Ron Jackson
Dan Jansen
Gregor Jelonek
John Jewell
Claudia Jiff
Sandy Johnson

Phil and Parker
 Johnston
Suma Joshua
Jared Joynt
Gilmore Junio
Yuri Kadobnob
Mark Greenwald
Darlene Kastner
Kyla Kastner
Walter Keifer
Mick Kiddle
Kameron Kiland
Frank King
Jeff Kitura
Cindy Klassen
Heinz Kluetmeier
Mark Knoll
Brad Kowal
Jeremy Kozuback
Alanna
 Kraus-Handley
Karrie Kreutz
Kristen Kunze
Elaine Kupser
Joachim Kuzel
Robert Laberge
Leah Lacroix
Marcel Lacroix
Kirsti Lay
Catriona Le
 May Doan
Ron Legere
Norm Lennon
John Little
Helen Louie
Penny Lye-Morelyle
Will MacDonald
Cam MacLeod
Liane MacNeil
Make-A-Wish-
 Foundation
Lucas Makowsky
Neal Marshall

Terry Masikewich
Sean Maw
Tom McCaffrey
Jim McClements
Todd McClements
John McClennan
Mark McGee
Caprice McGonigal
Alan McIlveen
Gail McLeod
Donald McSwiney
Carol Meibock
David Menary
Mark Messer
Diane Miller
Dustin Miller
Shannon Miller
David Mol
Alex Molotsky
James Monson
Denny Morrison
Noriko Munekata
Jo-Ann Munn Gafuik
Miwako Muraoka
Lynda Murch
Werner Myer
Christine Nesbitt
Greg Neufeld
Ken Newans
Bob Niven
NUTV
Hugh O'Neil
Olympic Oval Staff
Organizing
 Committee Calgary
Rob Owen
Cecilia Pacanins
Thomas Pacina
Crispin Parkinson
Wayne Parro
Wille Pavlinec
Laura Pedersen

Casey Peirce
Ollie Penguin
Doug Pensinger
Crystal Phillips
Gregg Planert
Stacey Polet
 (Crockett)
Cathy Priestner
 Allinger
Mengyao (Maggie) Qi
Andrew Quinn
Peter Reath
Mary-Ann Reeves
Ian Regier
Ryan Remiorz
Gillian Richmond
Paul Rickard
Mike Ridewood
Maria Robinson
Ronald McDonald
 House® Southern
 Alberta
Clive Rose
Royal Canadian Mint
Richard Sailer
Klaas Schipper
Kevin Scott
Jerry Search
Lynne Searles
Gladys Serafino
Colleen Seto
Torsten Silz
Janice Smith
Travis Smith
Shivani Sodha
Ruth Sorrentino
Speed Skating
 Canada
Speedskating
 online.com
Speedskating
 Results.com
Lynda Stauffer

Ben Stevenson
Tracy Stewart
Jo Ann Stimpson
Dave Stinton
Street Characters Inc.
Christopher Strong
Sun Media
 Corporation
Hutton Supancic
Eva Sy
Sylvie Tanguay
Christa Taylor
 Brothers
Taylor Family
 Digital Library
Magne Teigen
Hans Terstappen
Nol Terwindt
The Canadian Press
The Globe and Mail
Cara Thibault
Jacques Thibault
Dave Thompson
John Thorpe
Keith Toupin
Shawna Trudel
Yves Trudell
University of
 Calgary, Archives
University of Calgary,
 Copyright Officer
University of
 Calgary, Dinos
 Athletics
University of
 Calgary, Faculty
 of Engineering
University of
 Calgary, Faculty
 of Kinesiology
University of
 Calgary, Gauntlet
University of
 Calgary, Gazette

University of
 Calgary, Legal
 Services
University of
 Calgary, UToday
Johan van den
 Heuvel
Froukje van Dorssen
Rob van Grinsven
Scott Van Horne
Ivonne Vargas
Mojra Vaughn
Dr. Joan Norma
 Vickers
ViewCalgary
David Vink
Jeff Vinnick
Edwin Visser
Dusan Vranic
Wendy Walker
April Walters
Jack Walters
Xiuli Wang
Justin Warsylewicz
Jim Wells
Chris Welner
Diane Wensel
Jeff White
Roy Whitney
Hayley Wickenheiser
Georg Wiig
Mark Wild
Jock Wilson
Bill and Sharon
 Wotherspoon
Jeremy Wotherspoon
Adrian Wyld
John Yallop
Andy Yardy
Chuck Young
Selina Zaluski (Elm)

Photo Index

Autographs

Autographs